TRANSACTIONS

of the

American Philosophical Society

Held at Philadelphia for Promoting Useful Knowledge

VOLUME 74, Part 3, 1984

Eucharistic Presence and Conversion in Late Thirteenth-Century Franciscan Thought

DAVID BURR

Professor of History, Virginia Polytechnic Institute and State University

THE AMERICAN PHILOSOPHICAL SOCIETY

Independence Square, Philadelphia

1984

Library of Congress Catalog
Card Number 83-73283
International Standard Book Number 0–87169–743–2
US ISSN 0065–9746

CONTENTS

PREFACE

The following study concentrates on a single problem in medieval theology: the relationship between Christ's bodily presence in the eucharist and the conversion of the eucharistic elements, bread and wine, into Christ's body and blood. It traces discussion of this problem within the Franciscan order during the late thirteenth century from Saint Bonaventure to John Duns Scotus.

On the face of it, the project would seem to attain an almost heroic irrelevance. Why should one invest so much space in such an obscure topic? The ultimate answer to questions of this sort must always be sought in the recesses of the individual scholar's soul rather than in logical explanation, but in this case the investment of space (and, I fear, of considerable time) can be defended.

Certainly no one can deny the central importance of the eucharist in medieval piety. Nor can one deny that the truly stupendous claim made concerning it, namely, that Christ was physically present there, raised some thorny questions. In an age given to rational explanation as the thirteenth century was, such questions had to be faced. Within the Franciscan order, they were confronted in such a way as to illuminate, not only the gravity of the particular problem, but also the nature of the whole theological enterprise in the heyday of medieval scholasticism.

I shall begin by examining one view of this problem which is sufficiently enticing to have found acceptance among a large number of Roman Catholic theologians right down to the present. For reasons which will become obvious enough as the study progresses, I shall call this view the Thomist-Bonaventuran thesis. After showing the extent to which the view was endorsed within the church during the later thirteenth century, I shall chronicle its rejection within the Franciscan order by a series of theologians culminating in John Duns Scotus, whose positive formulation offered a strong alternative to the Thomist-Bonaventuran thesis.

Scotus will receive a notably larger share of attention than the others. Such treatment is merited, not only by his fame, but by the quality of his thought. It will be obvious as we progress that Scotus, far from reshaping the whole sorry scheme of things entire on the basis of a completely original appraisal of eucharistic theology, actually moved within a definable tradition shaped by previous Franciscan scholars. Nevertheless, I hope it will be equally obvious that, even when Scotus's originality has been reduced to its proper dimensions, his contribution remains awe-inspiring.

The difference between the Thomist-Bonaventuran thesis and the Scotist view is hardly unexplored territory for modern scholars.[1] Little has been done, however, to explain how (or even if) lesser scholars in the final decades of the thirteenth century provided a transition from one to the other. Such an omission seems understandable enough. It should surprise

---

[1] See David Burr, "Scotus and Transubstantiation," 34: 336–50.

no one that research on medieval theology tends to concentrate on major figures like Bonaventure, Aquinas, and Scotus. In addition to being more significant than minor figures, major ones are usually brighter and thus a good deal more fun to work on. Moreover, anyone who chooses to examine such luminaries can count on a rich bibliography of secondary sources and printed editions of primary sources which, if not always satisfactory, are at least readily available. The investigator of minor scholars will, if he is lucky, find himself making frequent trips to major American libraries in order to use early editions undiscovered by Kraus or Bert Franklin. If he is less fortunate, he will spend his time collating manuscripts.

Nevertheless, complete avoidance of lesser theologians can produce some odd results. When Aquinas and Scotus are made to face one another across the decades like gunfighters on a long, deserted western street, with no hint that the intervening years were filled with continuous debate and development, one's scholarship is apt to take on a disturbingly ahistorical tinge. At worst, such a method can lure an unsuspecting researcher into the sort of faux pas which lies in wait for those who, ignoring the historical context, treat medieval theologians as disembodied minds.[2] At best, it encourages them to overvalue the originality of major figures and underrate the cumulative effect of ongoing discussion within the intellectual communities from which an Aquinas or a Scotus arose.

The major contribution of this study lies precisely in its attention to secondary figures who taught within the Franciscan order after Bonaventure had surrendered his magisterial post and before Scotus had assumed his. I shall not cover all of these figures, but I will deal with as many as human fallibility and limited manuscript sources allow. If the two chapters primarily devoted to them are the most important in the entire work, they may also be the most tedious, since attention to each theologian as a discrete entity inevitably entails a fair amount of repetition. I see no way around this problem, however, and have tried to counterbalance the atomizing tendency of those chapters by providing a general overview in the conclusion.

The list of those who have contributed to this study is a long one, and most the people to whom I owe thanks must go unmentioned here. Since the work is based largely on manuscript sources, it could not have been written without the cooperation of those European libraries mentioned in the bibliography. In addition, I owe a particular debt of gratitude to *Mediaeval Studies* for allowing me to reprint large segments of my 1971 article on Scotus and to Virginia Polytechnic Institute and State University for financial aid.

---

[2] As a mild example one might cite Edith Sylla, "Autonomous and Handmaiden Science," 349–96. Sylla's suggestion (p. 377) that external factors like the institutional framework in which Aquinas and Ockham worked could not have had much influence on their respective views of the autonomy of philosophy because "both Aquinas and Ockham produced their commentaries on the *Sentences* in essentially the same institutional framework, that, namely, of the medieval university," seems to ignore a great deal that was going on in such universities during the half-century that separated the two commentaries. Moreover, this distortion is transmogrified into error by one of the discussants who, following Sylla's paper, interprets her as saying that "Thomas Aquinas and William of Ockham were both members of the same institution, the university of Paris" (p. 391).

I. THE COMMON HERITAGE

It is a truism that the process of selection necessary for any historical investigation involves some distortion of events as they actually occurred. The present study is no exception. In beginning with Bonaventure and Aquinas, it inevitably casts over their eucharistic thought an appearance of novelty which does not do justice to their participation in an ongoing, developing eucharistic tradition. Certainly Bonaventure and Aquinas did make a contribution, and in the fourth chapter we will see how important that contribution was. Nevertheless, their formulations were guided by implicit and even explicit acceptance of several factors as "given." Common sentiment within the church already had placed significant limitations upon the way a theologian in their day might understand the nature of Christ's eucharistic presence.

In the first place, Bonaventure and Aquinas, like other thirteenth-century theologians, began by assuming that Christ was physically present in the eucharist. Moreover, ever since the Berengarian controversy this general belief in Christ's physical presence had been given clearer outlines by a series of secondary affirmations. On the one hand, as the confession submitted to Berengar in 1079 clearly indicates, the body of Christ present in the eucharist was affirmed by the orthodox to be the same body which was born of the Virgin Mary, suffered on the cross and ascended into heaven to sit at the right hand of the Father.[1] Henceforth the confession of Berengar would help to guard against any interpretation of eucharistic presence which seemed to compromise its realistic character. On the other hand, that it was the body of Christ which was present carried with it another set of demands which needed attention. If realistic modes of expression had their uses, they also had their limitations. Here again the Berengarian controversy was central. The confession which Berengar had been forced to read in 1059 exceeded all reasonable limits in its assertion that the body of Christ was "broken by the hand of the priest and ground by the teeth of the faithful," and Guitmund, one of Berengar's most astute critics, anticipated later developments by arguing against any rending of the body on the ground that it is completely present in every piece of the host.[2] Although literal acceptance of the 1059 assertion was not unheard

---

[1] A. J. MacDonald, *Berengar and the Reform of Sacramental Doctrine* is still a very useful examination of the entire controversy, although recent authors have contributed substantially to our knowledge of limited aspects. See, for example, Jean de Montclos, *Lanfranc et Berenger*; Margaret Gibson, *Lanfranc of Bec.*

[2] Guitmund of Aversa, *De corporis et sanguinis Christi veritate,* in *PL,* 149, col. 1500. Guitmund was hardly the first to argue for the inviolability of Christ's body in the eucharist, however.

of,[3] both the affirmation of Christ's full presence in each segment and the
affirmation of inviolability so closely connected with it seem to have been
accepted as axiomatic by the great thirteenth-century scholastics, although,
as we shall see, there was still room for disagreement as to whether Christ
was related to the host in the same way before and after it was broken.

If Bonaventure and Aquinas were sure that Christ was really present,
they were equally sure that the substances of bread and wine were not.
Here the situation is complicated because the opposite notion exercised a
strong attraction throughout the Middle Ages; yet belief that the substance
of bread and wine ceased to exist was so widespread that in the late
thirteenth century Albert the Great could refer to the opposite view as
having no supporters.[4]

This general agreement on the disappearance of the substance of bread
and wine was closely tied with agreement that the bread and wine were
converted into Christ's body and blood. The idea of substantial conversion,
already expressed in the confession submitted to Berengar in 1079, was
fully accepted by Thomas's and Bonaventure's time and had been given
an official name, *transsubstantiatio*, by the Fourth Lateran Council in 1215.[5]

Mention of such terms as "substance" and "transubstantiation" suggests
another area in which Bonaventure and Aquinas were heavily dependent
upon their predecessors. They inherited not only a common store of beliefs
but a common set of terms in which those beliefs might be expressed and
by which they might even be clarified. Here again, the Berengarian controversy was of central importance. Although use of the terms "substance"
and "accident" antedates the controversy, application of such terms to the
issues at hand by Berengar's opponents contributed heavily toward definition of the role these terms would play in following centuries. The
twelfth century, building on the terminology and affirmations bequeathed
to it by the eleventh, saw extensive use of the idea of subsistent accident
or *accidens sine subiecto* and institution of the term *transsubstantiatio* to
describe eucharistic conversion. By the thirteenth century, both had become
part of the standard terminology utilized in eucharistic theology.[6]

See MacDonald, *Berengar*, 348. For a historical analysis of both the confession and the way
the church gradually came to terms with it, see Ludwig Hödl, "Die confessio Berengarii von
1059," 370–94.

[3] See Abbaud, *Tractatus de fractione corporis Christi*, in *PL*, 166, col. 1347f.

[4] *Commentarii in quartum librum sententiarum*, d. 11, a. 8, in *Opera*, Paris, Ludovicus Vivès,
1894, 29: 287.

[5] *Conciliorum Oecumenicorum Decreta*, Bologna, Herder, 1962, 206: Iesus Christus, cuius
corpus et sanguis in sacramento altaris sub speciebus panis et vini veraciter continetur,
transsubstantiatis pane in corpus et vino in sanguinem potestate divina, . . .

[6] See MacDonald, *Berengar*, 159, 342–44, 359 and elsewhere; Charles E. Sheedy, *The
Eucharistic Controversy of the Eleventh Century* 81ff. and 93ff.; Germain C. Williams, *The Nature
of the Eucharistic Accidents*, 35–37 and elsewhere; Raymond G. Fontaine, *Subsistent Accident
in the Philosophy of Saint Thomas and his Predecessors*; Burkhard Neunheuser, *Eucharistie in
Mittelalter und Neuzeit*, 27f.; Ludwig Hödl, "Der Transsubstantiationsbegriff in der scholastischen
Theologie des 12. Jahrhunderts," 230–59; H. Jorissen, *Entfaltung der Transsubstantiationslehre
bis zum Beginn der Hochscholastik*.

While the most important terms to which Bonaventure and Aquinas fell heir were already being used in the eleventh and twelfth centuries, it was their own century which gave these terms the depth and complexity which Bonaventure and Aquinas themselves utilized. Certainly words like "substance" and "accident" were available for use by philosophers and even by nonphilosophers before the entire Aristotelian corpus became available to the west in the twelfth and thirteenth centuries. Besides the nontechnical uses which such words might have acquired, more technical uses were available through familiarity with Aristotelian logic, and transition from a logical to a metaphysical use of these terms was not impossible. Nevertheless, it was in the thirteenth century that such words, already enriched by the new translations of the Aristotelian logical corpus in the twelfth, were given even greater significance by the gradual assimilation of Aristotelian physics and metaphysics. However one may feel about the long-standing dispute over "Aristotelian" and "Augustinian" philosophy in the thirteenth century, it is clear that Aristotelian philosophical terminology had become a standard tool for theologians by the second half of the thirteenth century and that not only Aquinas but Bonaventure felt obliged to come to terms with it.

Bonaventure and Thomas inherited not only a philosophical terminology derived from the gradual rediscovery and appropriation of Aristotelian philosophy, but a theological method which paralleled that rediscovery in growth and perhaps antedated it in genesis, a method which found its expression in the form of the *Sentence* commentary and *Summa.* Here theology was approached through the investigation of particular problems presented in the form of *quaestiones.* These *quaestiones* were approached in turn through utilization of the *sic et non* method in which divergent solutions were cited and evaluated. In the great scholastics, we see a tendency to mold this basic structure into an efficient argumentative form in which a *videtur* section led off with a series of arguments for the wrong solution, was countered with a brief *contra* section offering a different view, then was followed by a *respondeo* or *dicendum* section in which the author stated and defended his own position, the whole *quaestio* then being capped by a final barrage of arguments refuting those of the original *videtur* section. The entire structure was animated by desire for a clear, systematic presentation of the faith and its *rationes* so far as they might be discovered.

While it is hard to generalize about the motives with which the great thirteenth-century scholastics approached theology or the use they made of Aristotelian philosophy, it is safe to say that the stature Aristotle had gained in medieval learning made it inevitable that his philosophy should influence not only the terminology but the spirit in which subjects like eucharistic presence were discussed. Moreover, given the terminology and spirit, a whole series of questions followed almost inevitably. In the case of eucharistic presence, these questions were not entirely new. Since, as Thomists like to observe, there is more than a slight connection between Aristotelian philosophy and common sense, the question with which the thirteenth-century scholastics wrestled already had appeared in various forms in the works of older theologians. Nevertheless, a renascent Aristotelian philosophy could now be used as a precision instrument with which these questions might be given the sharpest possible point. The discussion could be carried on with an exactitude unknown to previous centuries.

Viewed in retrospect, the problems discussed seem straightforward, clear, and inevitable. Three basic types of questions had to be answered. First, there were those arising from the understanding of Christ's presence inherited by thirteenth-century theologians. If the body of Christ present in the eucharist is identical with the one born, executed, and resurrected in Palestine in the first century and now sitting in heaven, then the same body must be completely present in several places at once. In fact, according to accepted doctrine, it must be fully present not only in heaven but in every part of every eucharistic element on every altar where the sacrament is performed. Is this assertion not patently self-contradictory?

Again, if Christ is completely present, then he must be there with his normal accidents, including size, color, odor, and the rest. Why, then, can we not see, touch or smell him? How can a body over five feet tall be present in a tiny morsel of bread?

Again, complete presence would seem to entail possession of one's normal active and passive powers. If so, then do those who partake of the eucharist not subject Christ to a more agonizing ordeal than he suffered on the cross?

Second, there were questions regarding the nature of eucharistic conversion. If, as the name "transubstantiation" implies, the entire substance of bread is converted into the entire substance of Christ, is there no common element binding the two extremes of the conversion, as is the case in normal conversion when two forms succeed one another in a common matter? If there is indeed no common element, then is the idea of transubstantiation really distinguishable from that of the annihilation of one substance and the creation of another?

Again, there would seem to be two conversions, one after the other, successively involving the bread and the wine. In one case the words of institution explicitly mention Christ's body, while in the other they explicitly allude to his blood. How does this fact square with the assertion that Christ is fully present in each of the eucharistic elements?

Again, there is the question of why the doctrine of transubstantiation came to be accepted by theologians and was finally made dogma by the Fourth Lateran Council. After all, it does not seem to be demanded by the Bible. Is it, then, a necessary deduction from the affirmation of faith that Christ is present in the eucharist, or is transubstantiation itself an item of faith logically demanded by no other affirmation?

Finally, there were questions concerning the remaining accidents. Is the idea of accidents without a subject self-contradictory, violating the very definition of an accident? Granting that the notion is logically acceptable and that the accidents of bread and wine really do exist without a subject in the eucharist, what active and passive powers can they possess?

Given the common faith of the thirteenth century on the one hand and its common philosophical and theological predilections on the other, such questions had to be faced. Some modern Roman Catholic historians have suggested that the resultant eucharistic theology was a mixed blessing for the church, since increased speculation concerning such matters caused theologians to neglect serious consideration of the mass as sacrifice or cultic event.[7] It would be hard to dispute such a claim; yet we cannot thereby deduce that the speculation was wasted effort. Scholastic interest in the nature of Christ's eucharistic presence was at least partly motivated by apologetic needs. The orthodox doctrine of eucharistic presence was particularly vulnerable to the taunts of unbelievers and heretics alike, a fact which hardly escaped the notice of theologians.[8]

It is not hard to guess why heretics and non-Christians should have lavished attention on the doctrine. As we have seen, it contained some astounding claims. Moreover, it was absolutely central to medieval piety. As reverence for the eucharistic elements increased in the twelfth and thirteenth centuries, conceptual difficulties presented by the docrine became an increasingly more inviting target for enemies of the Catholic church, thus calling for ever more effective defenses by the faithful.

The apologetic dimension of thirteenth-century eucharistic theology is easily overlooked, since it is an element rather successfully suppressed by the theologians themselves. When William of Militona refutes the objection that successive eucharistic conversions would have a cumulative effect, eventually making Christ's body immense, he could well be dealing with an argument offered by the Cathari, but we would never learn that fact from William, who is interested in the argument's philosophical validity rather than its pedigree.[9] The scholastic theologian's tendency to avoid contemporary reference and view such matters *sub specie aeternitatis* gives his work a rather cloistered air, leaving us with the impression that his study was located a good deal farther up in the ivory tower than was actually the case.

Of course, not all challenges came from outside the Catholic church. Philosophical speculation within the universities often led to conclusions which seemed dangerous to the faith, and eucharistic doctrine had a way of popping up in this context. In fact, at no time did the problem seem more acute than during the period covered by this study. Our period

---

[7] See, for example, Erwin Iserloh, "Abendmahl und Opfer in katholischer Sicht," 78.

[8] See the comments concerning "rationalistic" criticism of eucharistic doctrine by heretics in Grado G. Merlo, *Eretici e inquisitori nella società piemontese del trecento*, 54 and 61, as well as the bibliography offered there.

[9] Guilelmus de Militona, *Quaestiones de sacramentis*, 676. I do not in fact know whether the Cathars used such an argument. They did use one with almost the opposite point, however: Si corpus domini nostri Ihesu Christi esset ita magnum sicut mons, modo esset comestum. See Yves Dossat, "Les cathares dans les documents de l'inquisition," 79.

includes the two condemnations of 1270 and 1277 by Stephen Tempier, bishop of Paris,[10] the parallel action in 1277 by Robert Kilwardby, archbishop of Canterbury,[11] and the mopping-up operations at Oxford attempted in the 1280s by Kilwardby's successor, John Pecham.[12]

No less than three of the philosophical positions attacked in this flurry of episcopal censures would seem to bear on the eucharist. Of the 219 propositions condemned at Paris in 1277, four deny that accidents can exist without a subject, thus challenging what we will soon see was eucharistic orthodoxy at that time.[13] One of the four also denies that more than one set of dimensions can coexist in the same place, a view which, as will be seen later, also seems to challenge the accepted notion of Christ's sacramental presence.[14] Finally, both Kilwardby and Pecham attack the notion that there is a single form in man.[15] In doing so, they reflect a long-term battle which had been going on throughout the 1270s and continued through the 1280s thanks to the *Correctorium* controversy, which pitted Thomas Aquinas's Franciscan detractors against his Dominican defenders. Here again, we will see that the battle was fought at least partly on the eucharistic front.

Clearly, then, speculation about Christ's eucharistic presence was encouraged by a variety of pressures inside and outside the Catholic church. The polemical function of eucharistic theology should not be overemphasized, however. Scholastic interest in the problem was inspired, not only by concrete dangers, but by the very dynamics of the scholastic enterprise. The primary responsibility placed upon theologians by that enterprise was not to prove the unprovable or explain the unexplainable—as Aquinas recognized, any such attempt could only invite ridicule[16]—but to talk sense, to use words responsibly. There was nothing wrong with affirming that eucharistic presence entailed one or more miracles. There was something very wrong in phrasing those miracles in sentences that violated the very meaning of the words used. The great scholastics did not shrink from the possibility that there was something supernatural about Christ's body being in several places at once, but they certainly wanted to counter the charge that it was flatly self-contradictory to say

---

[10] *Chartularium universitatis parisiensis,* 1: 486f. and 543–58.

[11] *Chartularium,* 1: 558f.

[12] *Ibid.,* 1: 624–27 and 634f. For an analysis of Tempier's actions see John F. Wippel, "The Condemnations of 1270 of 1277 at Paris," 169–201. For the English censures see D. A. Callus, *The Condemnation of St. Thomas at Oxford;* Decima Douie, *Archbishop Pecham,* chap. VIII.

[13] Roland Hissette, *Enquête sur les 291 articles condamnées à Paris le 7 Mars 1277,* 287–91 offers a discussion of these propositions and tries to discover thirteenth-century philosophers who held such a view. *Aegidius Romanus, Errores philosophorum,* 8f., 12f., 62f. and 66f. attributes the error both to Aristotle and to Maimonides.

[14] See Hissette, *Les 219 articles,* 287–91. The view is also censured by Aegidius Romanus, *Errores philosophorum,* 10–13.

[15] For the sustained attack on this doctrine by both men, see Frederick J. Roensch, *Early Thomistic School,* chap. IV.

[16] *Summa theologiae,* 1 q. 46, a. 2.

that a single body was so present. They had no quarrel with the idea that only God could make accidents exist without a substance, but they were eager to show that the notion of *accidens sine subiecto* did not defy the very definition of an accident. Otherwise their affirmations would have been, not right or wrong, but merely nonsensical.

When we observe the late thirteenth-century theologians attempting to come to terms with such problems, we recognize that they needed no pressure from outside the Catholic camp to keep them attentive to the questions involved. Their strongest motivation was their own inner integrity as intellectuals. As scholars, they felt an obligation to face difficult questions squarely. As Christians, they faced them with a confidence born from their conviction that the truth or falsity of the dogmas involved did not ultimately depend upon their ability to provide convincing arguments.

II. THE THOMIST-BONAVENTURAN THESIS

The combination of Bonaventure's name with that of Thomas Aquinas is a bit ironic when we consider that, in the later thirteenth century, Bonaventure was effusively praised by the same Franciscan scholars who felt Thomas's works needed correction before they could be used with any degree of security. Nevertheless, in the matter to be examined in this study, the two scholars spoke in unison. We will begin by looking at Bonaventure.

Bonaventure's chronology remains a well-chewed bone of contention among modern scholars,[1] and the best one can say at the moment is that he read the *Sentences* at Paris in the late 1240s or early 1250s. Thus his *Sentence Commentary* as we know it undoubtedly has its roots somewhere in that period, although he could have revised it during his *magisterium*, which came to an end in 1257 with his election as minister general of the Franciscan order.

Bonaventure's commentary on the *Sentences* is a rich, sprawling affair which covers all aspects of the eucharist. Here we shall limit ourselves to what, for our author, would be only a limited aspect of the subject, the relationship between Christ's presence and the conversion of bread and wine into his body and blood. The matter is first encountered in a question on whether Christ is truly in the sacrament.[2] Here Bonaventure raises the objection that presence of a thing where it formerly was not involves change (*mutatio*). The change involved cannot be local, since if it were such the body would leave heaven; yet it cannot be any other type of change, since all other varieties fall within the categories of *mutabile* and *alterabile*, which are impossible for a glorified body. Second, Bonaventure cites the objection that nothing can be outside the limit (*terminus*) of its substance. Since the body of Christ existing in heaven has the limit of its substance there, it cannot be elsewhere.

In the *conclusio* section, Bonaventure predictably affirms the established dogma of Christ's bodily presence. In response to the objection regarding change, he states that Christ is present through change in the bread converted into his body, not through change in his own body. As to the objection regarding limit, he notes that the body of Christ has its limit in heaven according to natural existence, but not according to the power of

---

[1] For a summary of previous opinions and the most recent contributions see John Quinn, "Chronology of St. Bonaventure (1217–1257)," 168–86; Theodore Crowley, "St. Bonaventure's Chronology Reappraisal," 310–22.

[2] *Sent.,* d. 10, p. 1, art. 1, q. 1, in *Opera*, Quaracchi, College of St. Bonaventure, 1891, Vol. IV.

conversion, through which a body can be converted into it elsewhere. These answers do not take one far into the problem, and Bonaventure promises to address the matter again later.

The problem next surfaces during Bonaventure's discussion of eucharistic conversion.[3] He cites Peter Lombard's observation that some people have posited a presence of Christ without any conversion, then rejects this position because it violates both reason and the authority of the *sancti*. As to the latter, Bonaventure does not specify, but earlier in the question he cites the biblical words *hoc est corpus meum,* commenting that "either the Truth speaks falsely or he converts the bread into Christ's body." He also cites Ambrose, Eusebius, Augustine, and John of Damascus.

Presence without conversion offends reason because it robs the sacrament of its truth, congruity, and utility. The sacrament is thus deprived of utility because, in seeking after probability and reason, the merit of faith is diminished. The congruity of the sacrament is decreased because the visible sacrament would not lead one to the body of Christ in the same way.

In what way does it rob the sacrament of its truth? Bonaventure refers back to an argument cited earlier in the question, according to which Christ must come to be present through some change (*mutatio*) either in himself or in something else. He is immutable in himself, so the only change one might imagine on his part is one of place, which involves change of the whole being in its integrity; yet change of place is ruled out because it entails leaving one place in order to attain another and excludes movement to two different places simultaneously. If Christ's eucharistic presence were based upon *mutatio secundum locum,* he could not remain in heaven and he could not become present on two altars at once through two simultaneous conversions. Thus we are left with the fact that Christ becomes present through a change in the bread, and Bonaventure assumes that this change is conversion.

In reply to the objection that such conversion would imply a steady increase in the size of Christ's body, Bonaventure protests that such would be the case if the bread were changed into a part of the body, but not if the whole were converted into the whole. In response to the objection that miracles should not be posited where they are not required, and the glorified body of Christ can be present along with the bread without a miracle, Bonaventure repeats his assertion that a miracle is posited here in accordance with the truth, congruity, and utility of the sacrament.

Once one has looked at the relevant passages in Bonaventure's sentence commentary, there is little left to examine. He does discuss the matter in his *Breviloquium,* which was probably composed during his period as a master (thus before 1257), but the passage is a brief one:

And because it was proper for Christ to be in these species because of alteration (*mutationem*) in the species and not in himself, thus, with the utterance of the aforesaid two-fold word in which Christ's existence under those species is suggested,

---

[3] Ibid., d. 10, p. 2, art. 2, q. 1.

there is a conversion of the substance of each into the body and blood of Christ, with only the accidents remaining as containing and expressive signs of the body.[4]

In contrast to Bonaventure, Thomas Aquinas never stopped discussing the issue of eucharistic presence, and he seldom spoke of the matter without touching upon the role of conversion. His recorded thoughts on the subject extend from his days as a *sententiarius* almost to the moment of his death. The earliest work in which he offers a systematic treatment of the real presence in his *Sentence* commentary, which was probably begun in Paris in 1252. Thomas had finished lecturing on the *Sentences* by the time he became a master in the spring of 1256, but we know that he continued to polish the commentary for at least a brief period after its inception.[5]

In this work, Thomas asks "whether the true body of Christ is contained in the sacrament of the altar," and answers, of course, that it is.[6] The interest of the question for our purposes lies in the way he responds to three objections raised in the *videtur* section. First, he imagines the objection that "nothing can be where it formerly was not without being changed." Thomas replies that it is not necessary for a thing to be changed when it begins to be present where it formerly was not, because it is possible for something to be converted into it. Since the body of Christ is present on the altar because the bread was converted into it, so that the whole body is the *terminus per se* of conversion, it is not necessary for it to be changed locally (*localiter motum*).

In response to the objection that no body can be in several places at once, Thomas notes that

no body is compared to a place except by the mediation of the dimensions of quantity, and thus a body is present as in a place where its dimensions are commensurated with those of the place. The body of Christ is present in this way in only one place, heaven. Since, however, the substance of bread is converted into the body of Christ; and since the bread was formerly in this place determinatively by the mediation of its dimension, which remain after transubstantiation has occurred; thus the place remains, but it is ordered to the body of Christ through the remaining dimensions of bread rather than through the dimensions of Christ's body . . . Thus it is not here as in a place speaking *per se*, but rather as in a sacrament not only signifying but containing it by the power of the conversion.[7]

---

[4] *Breviloquium,* in *Opera,* 5: 273 Et quia Christus sub illis speciebus esse debebat non secundum mutationem factam in ipso, sed potius, in eis; ideo ad prolationem duplicis verbi praedicti, in quo insinuatur existentia Christi sub speciebus illis, fit conversio substantiae utriusque in corpus et sanguinem, remanentibus solis accidentibus tanquam signis corporis contentivis et etiam expressivis.

[5] See James Weisheipl, *Friar Thomas d'Aqiuno,* 55–92 and 358f.

[6] *Scriptum super sententias,* Paris, Lethielleux, 1947, IV, d. 10, q. 1, a. 1.

[7] Ibid.: Nullum corpus comparatur ad locum nisi mediantibus dimensionibus quantitatis; et ideo ibi corpus est aliquod ut in loco, ubi commensurantur dimensiones eius dimensionibus loci; et secundum hoc corpus Christi non est nisi in uno loco tantum, scilicet in caelo. Sed quia conversa est in corpus Christi substantia panis, qui prius erat in hoc loco determinate mediantibus dimensionibus suis, quae manent transubstantiatione facta, ideo manet locus, non quidem immediate habens ordinem ad corpus Christi secundum proprias dimensiones,

Another objection argues that, if Christ can be in several places at once, he can be everywhere. Thomas answers that the body of Christ is said to be somewhere only by reason of its own dimensions or through the dimensions of that body which is converted into it. It is impossible for either to be ubiquitous, and thus the body of Christ cannot be such.

Finally, in response to still another objection, Thomas affirms that the body of Christ is in several places at once, not because it is glorified or united with divinity, but simply because it is the term of several conversions. Thus God could make a rock be in several places at once by the same means.

Later Thomas finds himself asking whether the bread remains after consecration.[8] Such a view, he says, is unfitting, impossible, and heretical. It is unfitting because it impedes the veneration due to the sacrament, for it would lead to idolatry if the veneration called *latria* were given to a host containing the substance of bread. Moreover, it would detract from the significance of the sacrament, for the species of bread and wine would not point to the body of Christ in the manner of a sign, but would point rather to the substance of bread. Finally, it would be contrary to the accepted use of the sacrament, since it would then be corporeal rather than purely spiritual food.

So far, we have been dealing only with the ways in which this notion is unfitting. It is also impossible, since

it is impossible for something to be in the present as it was not in the past unless it is changed or something is changed into it. Such could not even occur through a miracle, just as one could not be a mortal, rational animal without being a man; for to be in a different state in the present than in the past is the same as being moved or changed. Therefore, if the true body of Christ should now be present under the sacrament where it was not present earlier, some motion or change must intervene. No change occurs on the part of the bread according to this position. Therefore it necessarily follows that the body of Christ is changed at least in regard to place. . . . Such cannot be, however, because the body of Christ is consecrated in several places at once, and thus one body would have to be moved to different places at the same time. Such is impossible, since it would involve contrary motions (or at least different motions of the same species) existing simultaneously in the same thing.[9]

---

sed secundum dimensiones panis remanentes, sub quibus succedit corpus Christi substantiae panis. Et ideo non est hic ut in loco per se loquendo, sed ut in sacramento, non solum significante, sed continente ipsum ex vi conversionis factae.

[8] Ibid., d. 11, q. 1, a. 1.

[9] Ibid.: Sed quod sit impossibilis patet ex hoc quod impossibile est aliquid esse nunc cum prius non fuerit nisi ipso mutato vel aliquo in ipsum; nec posset etiam per miraculum fieri, sicut quod nec esset animal rationale mortale, et non esset homo; aliter enim se habere nunc et prius est idem quod moveri vel transmuteri. Si ergo corpus Christi verum esset sub sacramento nunc et non prius, oporteret aliquem motum vel mutationem intervenisse. Sed nulla mutatio est ex parte panis facta secundum hanc positionem. Ergo oportet quod corpus Christi sit mutatum saltem localiter, ut docatur quod corpus Christi est hic, . . . quod omnino esse non potest, quia cum simul et semel in diversis locis corpus Christi consecretur, oporteret quod simul et semel ad diversa loca unum numero corpus moveretur, quod est impossibile; quia

The position is heretical, because it contradicts the Bible. If the bread remained, one would have to say *hic est corpus meum* rather than *hoc est corpus meum*. This point is something more than an afterthought. Thomas makes it three times in the course of the discussion.

In the process of dispensing with objections, Thomas again returns to the logical contradictions involved in the view he is opposing. One of these objections states that the view in question (let us finally adopt the term "consubstantiation" and be done with it) is preferable because one should choose the view that offers less difficulties, and this one involves only the problem of two bodies in the same place, which is actually possible for a glorified body because of its subtlety (*subtilitas*). Thomas replies that consubstantiation involves, not less difficulties, but more and bigger ones, for it contains a clearcut self-contradiction. "It affirms a definition, namely 'being different now than in the past,' and yet cannot affirm the thing defined, which is change in the body of the lord or in the substance of bread."

Thomas now asks whether the bread is annihilated,[10] and replies that it is not, for "change (*motus*) is determined by the *terminus ad quem*." Thus the only change which can accurately be called "annihilation" is one in which the *terminus ad quem* is nothing. The *terminus ad quem* of the conversion in question is the body of Christ, "for nothing can begin to be present here where it formerly was not except through change (*motum*) in itself or in that which is terminated in it (*terminatam ad ipsum*)." If the bread were annihilated, then the body of Christ would not be the *terminus ad quem* of the conversion, and thus the change leading to Christ's presence would necessarily be in Christ himself, which we have seen to be impossible.

During the following decades, Thomas continued to discuss eucharistic presence in a series of Bible commentaries, quodlibetal questions and *summae*.[11] These works represent a deepening of the fundamental insights already present in the *Sentence* commentary. The result is seen in the tightly-woven argument of the *Summa theologiae*, Thomas's definitive statement on eucharistic presence.

---

contingeret simul contrarios motus inesse eidem, vel saltem diversos ejusdem speciei. A comparison of the Latin with my translation will illustrate the dangers of the vocabulary being employed and will, I hope, encourage the reader to watch the footnotes carefully. Words like *moveri* and *motus* are prime offenders. I sometimes translate them in accordance with the more general notion of change, at other times according to the more restricted notion of physical movement.

[10] Ibid., a. 2.

[11] The following works are worthy of examination:

Super Evangelium Matthaei Lectura, Taurini-Rome, Marietti, 1951, cap. 26 (written 1256–59).
Super Epistolas S. Pauli Lectura, Taurini-Rome, Marietti, 1953, cap. 11 (1259–65).
Super Evangelium S. Ioannis Lectura, Taurini-Rome, Marietti, 1952, cap. 6 (1269–72).
Qodl. 7, q. 4, aa. 1 and 3, in *Quaestiones Quodlibetales*, Taurini-Rome, Marietti, 1949, (1256).
Quodl. 9, q. 3, a. 1 (1258).
Quodl. 3, q. 1, a. 2 (1269).
Quodl. 5, q. 6, a. 1 (1271).
Summa contra gentiles, IV, cc. 63–67, in *Opera*, Rome, Typographia Polyglotta, 1918, XII (1258–64).

The *Summa theologiae* was begun in 1266, but the section on eucharistic presence was written in late 1272 or 1273, probably the latter.[12] Here even the structure of the work proclaims the centrality of conversion for Thomas's view. The normal order of the *Sentence* commentary, inherited from Peter Lombard and followed by Thomas himself as *sententiarius*, involved proceeding from the mode of Christ's presence to the manner of conversion and then finally to the nature of the remaining accidents. In the *Summa theologiae*, a work Thomas was freer to structure according to his own design, the order is changed. He begins with the nature of the conversion, then deals with the manner of Christ's presence.[13] This order mirrors the logical progression of his thought. For Aquinas, only he who understands eucharistic conversion can understand eucharistic presence.

Thomas establishes the impossibility of consubstantiation with a series of old, familiar arguments. If the bread remained, Christ could not be present, for a thing cannot be present where it formerly was not except by change of place or conversion of something into it. Clearly Christ cannot become present here by being moved locally, for he would then cease to be in heaven, would pass through all the intermediate places, and could end up in only one place at a time. Thus the bread must be converted into the body of Christ.

Moreover, consubstantiation would contradict the word *hoc est corpus meum*, which would have to be *hic est corpus meum*. Again, it would contradict the veneration given to the sacrament, for if there were another substance present besides the body of Christ it should not be given the worship of *latria*. Finally, it would call into question the rite of the church, which forbids the reception of Christ's body after consumption of corporeal food and yet permits one to partake of the sacrament twice.[14]

Annihilation is equally impossible, for it, too, would compromise the conversion necessary for eucharistic presence. Moreover, it is impossible to find any cause for such annihilation, since in a sacrament the effect should be signified by the form, and the words *hoc est corpus meum* cannot be taken to signify annihilation.[15]

Thomas is well aware that the conversion he posits is no ordinary conversion. Any natural change has a common subject which binds the two terms. Where does one find such a common subject when it is a case of converting one entire substance, form and matter, into another entire substance? If one can find none, how does such a conversion differ from annihilation of one substance and creation of another?[16]

---

[12] See Weisheipl, *Friar Thomas d'Aquino*, 360–62.

[13] This change in order is also found in the *Summa contra gentiles*.

[14] *Summa theologiae*, III, q. 75, a. 2. Texts of the *Summa theologiae* are legion. Perhaps the most accessible good one is the Blackfriars edition, London, Eyre and Spottiswoode, 1964, the eucharistic section being found in Vol. 58.

[15] Ibid., a. 3.

[16] This problem has a long prehistory in Thomas's writings. In IV *Sent.*, d. 10, q. 1, a. 4 he treats the terms in which eucharistic conversion can be expressed. This topic was considered very much *de rigeur* by late thirteenth-century theologians, who dutifully followed Peter Lombard's lead in pondering whether it was proper to say "what is bread will be the body

Thomas agrees at one point that there is indeed no subject, but suggests in another place that this conversion is, in a sense, in each of the substances, bread and body, as in a subject since the conversion entails a certain order of substances.[17] Elsewhere he suggests that the remaining accidents of bread and wine bear some resemblance to a subject.[18] These comments hardly add up to an energetic discussion of the matter, yet they show his recognition of what later scholars would treat as a problem area.

Having dealt with the nature of eucharistic conversion, Thomas turns to the manner of Christ's presence. His argument unfolds neatly from two basic distinctions, both of them related to his notion of conversion. The first, already present in the *Sentence* commentary,[19] is that between presence by the power of the sacrament (*ex vi sacramenti*) and presence by natural concomitance. That which comprises the immediate term of conversion is present in the former way, while everything inseparably related to it is present in the latter.

The second distinction, that between presence in the manner of a substance (*per modum substantiae*) and presence in the manner of quantity, was not really exploited by Thomas in the *Sentence* commentary,[20] yet it follows from the first distinction. Since the eucharistic conversion is one of substance into substance and not of accidents into accidents, only the substance of Christ's body is present *ex vi sacramenti*. The accidents are present by natural concomitance. Thus Christ is present in the manner of substance and not in the manner of quantity. The whole nature of a substance is contained in a quantity of any size, be it tiny or gigantic. The whole nature of man, for example, is contained in a large or small man. The whole Christ, substance and accidents, is thus present in the eucharist.

Apply these distinctions to the eucharist and apparently commonsense objections begin to disappear. Since Christ is present in the manner of a substance, there is nothing odd about such a large body fitting into such a small space. Nor is there anything amiss about the entire body being present in each part of the species, for the entire nature of a substance is present under any part of the dimensions containing it. Nor should we wonder that we cannot see Christ, for the accidents by which we would normally perceive his substance are present in the eucharist only through natural concomitance and in the manner of substance. Thus Christ's body remains an organic whole with its parts distributed in the normal manner,

---

of Christ," "bread becomes the body of Christ," etc. Insufferably tedious as such discussions may seem, Thomas and others recognized that they raised a fundamental question: What sort of link binds together the two termini of the conversion? In IV *Sent.* Thomas meets the issue head-on by announcing that the eucharistic conversion differs from all other *mutationes* inasmuch as there is no common subject, but only two *termini*.

[17] *Summa theologiae*, III, q. 75, a. 4.

[18] Ibid., aa. 5 and 8. Compare his argument in *Summa contra gentiles*, IV, c. 63.

[19] See IV *Sent.*, d. 10, q. 1, a. 2.

[20] It took shape soon after, however. See Super *Evangelium Matthaei Lectura*, cap. 26; *Super Epistolas S. Pauli Lectura*, cap. 11.

but these parts are not related to the place where they are present in such a way that they can be seen, touched, or directly affected in any way.

We have reached the point where a few general comments on Bonaventure and Aquinas are in order. Certainly there are differences. Thomas took a lifetime to develop his position, and his final formulation shows that his time was hardly wasted.[21] On the whole, however, once one allows for the greater sophistication of Thomas's later position and for minor terminological differences, the basic resemblance is striking. Both Thomas and Bonaventure distinguish between eucharistic presence and presence through the mediation of dimensions. Both distinguish between what is present precisely through the conversion and what is there because of its inseparable connection with the conversion.

More important for our purposes, they see eucharistic conversion as both an adequate explanation and a necessary explanation of eucharistic presence. It is an adequate explanation in the sense that, for Thomas and Bonaventure, Christ is present in the eucharist precisely because the bread and wine turn into his body and blood. For both men, the nature of the conversion influences the manner of Christ's presence, although Thomas goes much farther in this direction by applying the notion of presence in the manner of substance to a whole series of problems.

Eucharistic conversion is seen by both men as a necessary explanation of eucharistic presence in the sense that it provides, not only a cogent explanation of such presence, but the only one conceivable. In each case, the ways in which Christ can be present are limited to two, one of which is deemed impossible. From this perspective, consubstantiation and annihilation are ruled out, not only because they are contradicted by authority, but because they rob one of that single remaining alternative.

---

[21] Some differences, of course, stem more from temperament than from time and attention. Note, for example, the way Thomas and Bonaventure differ on what happens when a trespassing mouse eats the eucharistic host. Bonaventure, IV *Sent.*, d. 13, a. 2, q. 1; Aquinas, *Summa theologiae*, III, q. 80, a. 2. For the difference between Thomas and Bonaventure as perceived by other writers see J. Bittremieux, "De transsubstantiatione quid sentierit S. Bonaventura," 26–39; Fr. Kattum, *Die Eucharistielehre des heiligen Bonaventura.*

III. EUCHARISTIC THOUGHT IN THE 1240s: ALBERT THE GREAT, WILLIAM OF MILITONA, AND RICHARD FISHACRE

Such, then, are the thoughts of Thomas Aquinas and Bonaventure on the relationship between conversion and presence. However interesting these thoughts may be in themselves, it may not be all that evident to the casual observer that their historical significance is such as to merit the attention given them so far in this study. In order to weigh the achievement of Bonaventure and Aquinas, we must make at least some effort to place them in the context of eucharistic thought as it developed in the thirteenth century. Having done so, we will begin to appreciate both their debt to the ongoing scholastic tradition and their contribution to that tradition.

In lieu of a full-scale history of thirteenth-century eucharistic thought, I shall offer a survey of the 1240s, the decade immediately preceding Thomas's activity as *sententiarius* and perhaps even including Bonaventure's performance in that role. Three authors will be considered at length: Albert the Great, William of Militona, and Richard Fishacre. The order to be adopted here has little to do with chronology, which is vague enough in any case. Its true rationale will, I hope, become evident as the chapter progresses.

Albert the Great's views on the eucharist are expressed in two works spanning the 1240s.[1] In the first of these writings, the *De sacramentis,* which was written sometime in the early part of that decade, Albert approaches the problem of eucharistic presence by remarking that Christ's body must be considered in three ways. As the body of a person, it is to be thought of with its proper quantity and organization, united to the soul and to divinity. As head of the church, it has the same quantity, but this quantity is not to be thought of along with it. Third, it is to be considered as food for the mystical body, the church, and this is the important sense for the present discussion. The answer to all objections raised against Christ's eucharistic presence is that "the body of Christ is not related to those species as a placed thing to a place, or as a measured thing to

---

[1] For the dating of Albert's eucharistic writings see Wilhelm Kubel's prolegomena to the *De sacramentis* in *Opera,* Münster i. Westf., Aschendorff, 1958, Vol. 26, x; Albert Lang, "Zur Eucharistielehre des hl. Albertus Magnus," 124–32; Odon Lottin, *Psychologie et morale aux XIIe et XIIIe siècles,* 269–86. On the authenticity of the Albertine eucharistic works see also Franz-Josef Nocke, *Sakrament und personaler Vollzug bei Albertus Magnus,* 6–9. These citations represent only part of what has become a huge bibliography on the subject.

something which measures it, but as signified spiritual food to that which signifies it." Thus the body of Christ is not related to the species in such a way as to be larger or smaller than they are, for it is related to these forms only as a sign (*secundum solam rationem signi*), and a sign is equally in the whole and in each part.[2] The body is "a human-divine body feeding us spiritually, and, according as it feeds us, it is taken, not as a quantified thing, but as divine."

Two other elements are soon added to the explanation.[3] In the first place, "when certain causes are sufficient to induce an effect, that effect will be found wherever the causes are encountered." He goes on to say that "the proper form and matter are the sufficient causes of Christ's bodily presence in the sacrament," but he does not elaborate. One assumes that he is thinking of the words of institution pronounced over the bread and wine.

Second, "God is everywhere, while the creature is in one place. Thus something that has the properties of both . . . will be capable of being in several places." Albert goes on to specify that Christ is not on the altar as in a place (*ut in loco*), except *per accidens*.

The notion of Christ as spiritual food is important to Albert, and he makes telling use of it at least two more times in this *articulus* alone as he cuts his way through the various objections. To the objection that Christ's body is in a place circumscriptively and can therefore be in that place alone, he replies that "the body of Christ is only in heaven circumscriptively, but is on the altar as spiritual food in the manner of a type. Since there is a single relation to one and to many signs, Christ will be equally under one and many forms and on one and many altars."[4] When faced with the objection that even a spiritual nature, which is *simplicior* than a corporal one, is definitively in one place, Albert asserts that "Christ's body is related to the species, not insofar as it has corporeal dimensions, but insofar as it is simple and spiritual food, and from this perspective it is simpler than any spiritual creature considered in itself."[5]

Albert next treated eucharistic presence in 1249, when he composed the fourth book of his *Sentence* commentary. Here he begins, in the traditional order for such commentaries, with the question of whether Christ's body is really present on the altar. He counters the objection that what is immutable, neither gaining nor receiving anything, cannot be present

---

[2] *De sacramentis*, tractatus 5, pars 1, q. 4, a. 2: Unde patet, quod ipsum non est mensuratum aequale nec excellens nec diminutum, cum non referatur ad formas nisi secundum solam rationem signi, et quia una ratio est signi in toto et in partibus, propterea uno modo est sub toto et partibus.

[3] Ibid., a. 4.

[4] Ibid.: Ad primum ergo dicimus, quod corpus Christi circumscriptive non est nisi in caelo, sed in altari est ut cibus spiritualis in typo. Unde cum una sit relatio ad unum et plura signa, aequaliter erit sub una et sub pluribus formis et in uno et in pluribus altaribus.

[5] Ibid.: Ad alius: quod quantum ad dimensionem corporalem non est relatio corporis Christi ad formas, sed quantum ad rationem cibi simplicis et spiritualis, et in hac ratione simplicius est quam aliqua spiritualis creatura in se considerata.

through conversion of something else into itself.[6] Such is true, he says, of conversion according to one essential part of substance, as when the form is changed but not the matter. Here, however, the whole substance of bread becomes the whole substance of Christ's body, and thus the body "necessarily remains the same, but becomes present where such transsubstantiation occurs."

Another objection asserts that what is circumscribed in one place cannot be present in another without receding from its former location. Albert agrees that such is the case when one is dealing with things which are in place only definitively or circumscriptively. It is not true of Christ's body, which is related to place in two ways. In one of these ways it is present *per se* in its own form, is circumscribed in place, and its parts are related to individual parts of the place. In the other way it is related to the place through something else, such as the form of the host, and is entirely in all of that something else. If Christ became present in a new place in the former way, his body would necessarily recede from its old location, but such is not required when he becomes present in the second way.

A third objection protests that a spirit cannot be in several places at once, much less can a body do so. Albert notes that the ability to be in several places at once does not belong to a spirit insofar as it is a spirit, or to a body insofar as it is a body, but to Christ insofar as he works in himself and others. As related to himself he is in a place circumscriptively, but as related to others whom he unites with himself, he is present to them in the form of food.

Another objection suggests that, if Christ can be in several places at once, he can be everywhere at once. Such does not follow, Albert says. Christ is circumscriptively in one place and sacramentally in others. Since his sacramental presence involves relationship to the eucharistic species, it follows that his presence is limited to that finite number of places where the consecration takes place.

Two other objections are directed at the notion that Christ's divinity can serve as an explanation of his ability to be present in several places. In the process of countering them, Albert asserts that,

in order for Christ to be food converting us to himself, he must be united to divinity; and since, thanks to that fact, it is possible for him to be in several places where there are members of his body to be fed or already fed, some have said that the body can be in several places insofar as it is divine; and I concede that it has this power, not insofar as it is glorified, but insofar as it is food.[7]

Union with divinity "gives a body power which it did not have before, namely that of feeding spiritually; and thus such a body receives the ability

---

[6] *Commentarii in IV sententiarum,* In *Opera omnia,* Paris, Vivès, 1894, Vol. 29, IV, d. 10, a. 1.

[7] Ibid.: Ad hoc quod corpus Christi possit esse cibus nos ad se convertens, oportet quod sit divinitati unitum; et cum gratia illius conveniat ei esse in pluribus locis ubi sunt membra cibanda vel cibata, dixerunt quidam, quod in quantum divinum est corpus, habet quod possit esse in locis pluribus: et bene concedo, quod bene habet hoc: non in quantum est gloriosum, sed potius in quantum est cibus.

to be present in various places where there are members to be fed."[8]
Obviously Albert's interest in the eucharist as spiritual food has not diminished. In fact, he returns to the theme in succeeding articles, where it
is combined with the idea of the eucharist as sign.[9]

He affirms in straightforward fashion that the bread is not annihilated,
since it is converted into the substance of Christ's body.[10] Moreover, he
cites three arguments against consubstantiation. First, it would involve the
falsity of the words *hoc est corpus meum*. Second, the authorities are against
it. Third, it would rob the sacrament of its function as a sign, since the
accidents would direct the mind toward the substance of bread rather than
toward the invisible body of Christ.[11]

William of Militona's most substantial contribution to eucharistic thought
is his *Questions on the Sacraments*, a work considered by its modern editors
to have been written by 1249 and perhaps after 1245.[12] Two hundred
and eighty-seven pages of the *Questions on the Sacraments* are devoted to
the eucharist. Of these, forty-three deal with the nature of Christ's real
presence. Thus the section on eucharistic presence represents a considerable
part of an even more considerable document.

It is, in fact, more extensive than informative. William raises the question
of whether Christ is present in his full quantity, and answers that

in this sacrament, certain things are according to nature, others beyond nature but
not beyond understanding, and still others beyond understanding and nature.
Certain accidents such as color are there according to nature, as is the power of
such accidents to perform their natural actions. . . . It is beyond nature that the
accidents are there without a subject, . . . but this is not beyond understanding,
for by abstraction the intellect understands accidents without a subject. It is beyond
nature and understanding that Christ is there in the same quantity in which he
is in heaven, and yet does not exceed the boundaries of that tiny form.[13]

William denies an objection that parts would have to be there in confused
fashion, with the foot where the hand is. By supernatural power, the body
is there in its accustomed quantity and has part outside of part in the
usual manner.[14] This insight is supported by the narration of a eucharistic

---

[8] Ibid.: . . . ab ipsa unione confertur ei potentia quam non habuit, scilicet potentia cibandi
spiritualiter: et per consequens confertur ei, quod possit esse ubi cibanda membra sunt in
diversis locis.

[9] Ibid., d. 13, aa. 10–13.

[10] Ibid., d. 10, a. 7.

[11] Ibid., d. 10, a. 8.

[12] *Quaestiones de sacramentis*, Quaracchi, College of St. Bonaventure, 1961. For the date
see the prolegomena, pp. 5*–33*. Militona (or Melitona) probably means Milton.

[13] Ibid., p. 646: "Respondeo: in hoc sacramento quaedam sunt secundum naturam, quaedam
supra naturam, sed non supra intellectum, quaedam supra intellectum et supra naturam.
Secundum naturam sunt ibi accidentia quaedam, sicut color, sapor in magnitude, et aptitudo
accidentis respectu actus sui, sicut albedinis ad immutandum visum. Supra naturam sunt ibi
accidentia sine subiecto, ut color, sapor, rotunditas sine substantia. Hoc autem est supra
naturam, sed non supra intellectum, intelligit autem intellectus accidentia sine subiecto per
abstractionem. Supra naturam et intellectum est ibi Christus in tanta quantitate in quanta
est in caelo, et non excedit terminos illius parvulae formulae."

[14] Ibid., p. 647.

miracle and the matter is closed with the invocation of Innocent III's admonition that in this matter "we are commanded to believe and forbidden to discuss."[15]

Nevertheless, William's work is not entirely devoid of explanation. In pondering Christ's total presence in each part of the bread, he comments that the body, although physical, has a mode of presence similar to that of a spirit.[16] Note, he says, that corporeal created being not united with the divine is limited in such a way that, when it is contained in something, the whole is in the whole and the part in the part. Spiritual created being not united with divinity is not thus limited, and therefore the whole can be in the whole and in every part, as in the case of the soul's relation to the body; yet it is still limited insofar as it is in these parts only if they are united to the whole, and thus the soul cannot be in a part of the body separate from the rest. Finally, corporeal being united with the divine, like the body of Christ, is even less limited, for it can be entirely in the whole and in each part, whether these parts are united or separated; yet it is limited inasmuch as it cannot be present in this manner unless it is sacramentally present, and it cannot be everywhere as the divine nature alone can.[17]

William asks whether the bread is annihilated, and replies that annihilation has two meanings.[18] If it is taken to mean that nothing remains of what formerly was present and that what was present is changed into something else, then the term is apt. If it is taken to mean that nothing remains and there is no change into something else, then it is not so apt. In reply to the objection that in natural change the word "annihilation" applies if nothing remains of that which was formerly present, William affirms that this is because natural power cannot convert one being completely into another without something remaining as the subject of the action. Thus, if nothing remains of that which is changed, the action ceases and the thing cannot be changed into another but is simply annihilated. Such is not the case with supernatural power, however. In response to the objection that the mere presence of Christ's body following the disappearance of bread does not cause that disappearance, just as the generation of a new substance after the corruption of an old one does not cause that corruption, William insists that the bread would be annihilated only if the presence of Christ's body followed the disappearance of the bread in such a way that the latter was in no way converted into the former. Again, such is not the case. There is real conversion.

William deals with the possibility of consubstantiation very briefly in the process of asking what sort of change is involved in transubstantiation. While it is clear that the conversion involves no growth or nutrition,[19] the

---

[15] Ibid., pp. 647f. The reference is to *De sacro altaris mysterio*, IV, c. 8 (PL 217, p. 861).
[16] Ibid., p. 655.
[17] Ibid., pp. 654f.
[18] Ibid., pars 7, q. 35, pp. 659ff.
[19] Ibid., q. 36, pp. 668ff.

matter of *motus localis* is not so easy to settle.[20] Some say that, when the words of consecration are spoken, "the substance of the bread is consumed and the body of Christ is present." Others say that the substance of bread remains and the body of Christ becomes present with it in the same place, this being possible because the body of Christ is glorified. According to this view, Christ becomes present only by the power of the words of consecration. Both of these views assert that, by the power of the words, there is some change of place on Christ's part.

The third opinion is that the substance of the bread is converted into the substance of Christ's body with no change at all on Christ's part, even of place. This is the true view held by the church, which rejects the other two. To the objection that a body cannot be in diverse places without an intervening change of place, William replies that two things are involved in a change of place: That a thing be where it formerly was not, and that it not be where it formerly was. The first is found in the present case, but the second is not. Nevertheless, the same body cannot be in diverse places by natural power without the intervention of local motion.

The third and final author whom we will examine is the Dominican Richard Fishacre, whose brief career at Oxford was ended by what seems to have been an untimely death in 1248. While it is impossible to date his *Sentence* commentary precisely, there is good evidence that it was composed during the first half of the decade.[21]

During this examination of the eucharistic conversion, Richard ponders the classic alternatives of transubstantiation, annihilation, and consubstantiation.[22] The first, he says, posits only change of place, and this through the power of the sacrament. The second posits change of place and, in addition, corruption. The third seems to imply no change at all. As the Lombard says, the third alternative is contradicted by the overwhelming weight of authority. Moreover, if the third alternative were the case, there would be no miracle involved, since it is natural for a glorified body to be together with an unglorified body; yet the eucharist is one of God's most marvelous miracles. Again, if the bread remained, the priest would break his fast when he celebrated communion, and thus he could not celebrate again.

Fishacre rules the second alternative out because it would involve nothing more than a succession of two things, and thus any such succession could be called a conversion. Again, what would be so marvelous about the power of the words *hoc est corpus meum* if they produced nothing that was not already made and corrupted some good thing already in existence? Again, if the substance of bread is not converted into flesh, what would

[20] Ibid., q. 37, pp. 672 ff.
[21] See Franz Pelster, "Das Leben und die Schriften des Oxforder Dominikanerlehrers Richard Fishacre," 518–53; D. A. Callus, "Introduction of Aristotelian Learning at Oxford," 229–81.
[22] MS Oxford, Oriel 43, f. 365ra. I shall cite only this manuscript although I have compared it against Oxford, Balliol 57; Cambridge, Gonville and Caius 410 (329); and London, British Museum Royal 10 B 7.

be the point of its destruction, given the fact that both bread and body of Christ could exist in the same place? Thus, Richard says, scholars come down on the side of the first alternative.

The most interesting part of Fishacre's eucharistic thought is the way he handles the question of whether Christ is in various parts of the host and on various altars through his divinity or through the fact that his is a glorified body. To this question, Fishacre says, "I reply without assertion that neither glorification nor union with divinity is the reason why this body is in several places, but the cause of its being wholly in diverse altars under diverse species is the enunciation of the words . . . at diverse altars." The cause of his presence in various parts of the host after it is broken is, as we have seen, the indivisibility of Christ's body. If, then, neither glorification nor divinity are causes of Christ's multiple presence, "it seems that this could happen to Peter's body, that is, through the power of God's word, the bread could be transubstantiated into the body of Peter, and his body could be entirely present in many places."[23]

Fishacre deals with the questions of how a large body can be in such a small place and whether the parts of Christ's body are presented in confused fashion, yet he retains a strong sense of his own inability to answer such questions and is never more than provisional, despite intriguing discussions of the nature of glorified bodies and the way light is reflected in a mirror, both of which are offered as limited analogies. He does note that, "since bread is homogeneous, there is no more reason why this piece should be converted into Christ's hand than there is why that one should, and thus either every part of the bread is transubstantiated into the hand or none is."[24]

As one studies these three theologians of the 1240s, one begins to appreciate the extent to which Bonaventure and Thomas moved along well-trod paths. By their time, it was accepted practice to reject consubstantiation and anything except a rather attenuated sense of annihilation. Substantial conversion was *de rigeur*. One could add to the list of such common notions and demonstrate the extreme length of their pedigree in some cases, but there is no reason to do so.

At the moment, it is more important to note the area in which Albert, William, and Richard differed from Bonaventure and Aquinas: the relationship between eucharistic presence and eucharistic conversion. Of course, all three of the earlier theologians recognized some connection between the two ideas. It would have been extremely difficult not to do so. Nevertheless, this recognition could take various forms.

In Albert's case, the picture is an exceedingly complex one. He acknowledges that, through substantial conversion, "the body [of Christ] necessarily remains the same, but becomes present where such transubstantiation occurs."[25] He also seems to describe the words of institution

---

[23] Ibid., f. 371vb.
[24] Ibid., f. 372ra.
[25] *Sent.* IV, d. 10, a. 1.

pronounced over the elements as "the sufficient causes of Christ's bodily presence in the sacrament."[26] Thus he might seem to agree with Bonaventure and Aquinas that transubstantiation provides a sufficient explanation of Christ's eucharistic presence.

Upon closer inspection, this apparent agreement seems less firmly established. In the first place, the eucharistic consecration is not precisely the same as transubstantiation. One could at least imagine a theologian arguing that the words of consecration rather than transubstantiation effected eucharistic presence. In fact, those opting for consubstantiation or annihilation would do precisely that. Albert, of course, opts for neither, so the connection between consecration and conversion is a stronger one in his case. Nevertheless, the distinction remains.

More important, Albert may refer to transubstantiation as a factor in Christ's eucharistic presence, but he does not explore the connection very rigorously, nor does he place such weight on transubstantiation as to eschew all other possible explanations. In fact, there are other elements on which he lavishes a great deal more attention. Note, for example, his reliance on the ideas of Christ as sign and, more important, as food for the mystical body. The latter is clearly his favorite recourse when he finds it necessary to explain how the body of Christ can be in several places at once and entirely in each part of the host. Whereas Thomas argues that Christ is entirely in each part of the host because he is present in the manner of substance, and it is the nature of substance to be fully present in each part, Albert says that Christ is so present because he is there as spiritual food, and the same nature of food is in each part of the food as well as in the whole.

Albert also feels that Christ's divinity is an important part of the explanation. In fact, the element of divinity is closely related to Christ's role as spiritual food, for it is union with divinity which gives his body the power of feeding spiritually.[27]

William's case is also ambiguous. Recognition of a strong connection between conversion and eucharistic presence is implied by his use of the distinction between presence through the power of conversion and presence by natural concomitance[28] and by his way of setting up the alternatives of consubstantiation, annihilation, and conversion.[29] Here again, however, one finds no coherent attempt to explore the implications of substantial conversion as an explanation of the possibility and nature of eucharistic presence. On at least one occasion he asserts that it is beyond our understanding how Christ can be present in his complete corporeal quantity. Moreover, William has recourse to the notion that union with divinity allows a body to be entirely present to the whole and to each part.

Richard Fishacre seems the most promising of the three from a Bon-

---

[26] *De sacramentis*, a. 4.
[27] *Sent.* IV, d. 10, a. 1.
[28] *Qq. de sacramentis*, q. 39.
[29] Ibid., q. 37.

aventuran or Thomist point of view. It is he who argues that Christ is present in several places at once, not because he has a glorified body or because his body is united with divinity, but because the words of consecration are spoken in several places at once, and that Peter's body could be present in exactly the same way.[30] Thus he anticipates succeeding theologians in eliminating two explanations which had seen a good deal of service by his own time. Moreover, having focused attention on the consecration and, by implication, the conversion, he goes at least a part of the way toward explaining the nature of Christ's presence in terms of the conversion, arguing that, "since the bread is homogeneous, there is no more reason why this piece should be converted into Christ's hand than there is why that one should, and thus either every part of the bread is transubstantiated into the hand or none is." Nevertheless, he does not attempt to carry this approach through consistently as his fellow Dominican Thomas would do.

So far, we have examined Albert, William, and Richard in the light of the Bonaventuran and Thomist tendency to see transubstantiation as a sufficient explanation of eucharistic presence. When we turn to the other aspect of the Bonaventuran-Thomist position, conversion as a necessary explanation, the distinction between the two groups is clear. Whatever arguments Albert, William, and Richard may offer for transubstantiation over consubstantiation and annihilation, they never try to argue that rejection of transubstantiation would entail rejection of Christ's eucharistic presence, since the requirements of sacramental presence could be fulfilled only through the substantial conversion of something else into Christ's body.

---

[30] It might be noted for the record that appeal to Christ's glorified body as a factor determining the nature of his presence, although not seen in any of the works examined so far, was hardly a figment of Richard's imagination. It can be found in William of Auvergne's *De sacramentis, Opera omnia*, Paris, André Pralard, 1674, Vol. I, pp. 442–45. William cites the nature of a glorified body in his explanation of how Christ can be in such a small place, how he comes to be present instantaneously on the altar, and how he can be in several places at once, although in dealing with the latter question he also leans heavily on Christ's divinity.

IV. RECEPTION OF THE THOMIST-BONAVENTURAN THESIS OUTSIDE THE FRANCISCAN ORDER

We have seen that the Bonaventuran-Thomist view of transubstantiation as both a sufficient and a necessary explanation of eucharistic presence was not something they shared with the generality of scholars in their time, but seems rather to have been a significant contribution which they made to eucharistic thought. It is time to address ourselves to the question of how that contribution was received during the remaining decades of the thirteenth century. We will glance briefly at the Dominicans, other religious orders, and the secular masters before turning to the main subject of our study, the Franciscans.

It will hardly surprise anyone that the Bonaventuran-Thomist view made a positive impression on theologians within Thomas's own order. In fact, one would be astounded to discover that it was otherwise. Thus one is quite prepared to find Peter of Tarentaise, who lectured on the *Sentences* at Paris sometime between 1256 and 1259,[1] explaining that the quantity of Christ's body is present *mediante substantia* and arguing that consubstantiation and annihilation are both to be rejected because each would deny in its own way that substantial conversion which must occur if Christ is to be present in the sacrament.[2]

Not all Thomas's confreres followed his lead in this respect. Hugh of Strasbourg, writing between 1265 and 1270,[3] moves in the tradition of William of Militona when he argues that Christ's presence in several places at once is due to his union with divinity and exclaims that the presence of such a large body under such a small form is beyond our understanding.[4] Albert the Great's last word on the subject, the *Liber de sacramento eu-*

---

[1] See R. Creytins, "Pierre de Tarentaise, Professeur à Paris et Prieur Provincial de France," 73–100; H.-D. Simonin, "Les écrits de Pierre de Tarentaise," 163–335; M.-H. Laurent, *Le bienheureux Innocent V (Pierre de Tarentaise) et son temps*, 39–59, 361.

[2] Petrus de Tarantasia, *In IV libris senteniarum commentaria*, Toulouse, Arnoldus Colomerius, 1652, IV, d. 10, q. 1, a. 2, and d. 10, q. 2, a. 1. As Simonin, "Les écrits," 175–91, justly observes, Peter is following not only Thomas Aquinas but Bonaventure as well in his *Sentence Commentary*, and sometimes actually mediates between the two. Thus, in d. 13, q. 1, a. 6, he presents both opinions on what a mouse eats without attempting to decide which is correct.

[3] See Luzian Pfleger, "Der dominikaner Hugo von Strassburg und das Compendium theologicae veritatis," 429–40; Georg Bonner, "Uber den dominikaner theologen Hugo von Strassburg," 269–86.

[4] Hugo de Argentina, *Compendium theologicae veritatis*, caput 14, in Albertus Magnus, *Opera*, Paris, Vivès, 1895, 34: 213.

charistiae, which was written after 1260,[5] proceeds along much the same lines as his earlier writings. Albert's argument against consubstantiation, which he considers to be "not heretical, but very imprudent and quite close to heresy," is entirely innocent of any notion that conversion might be linked necessarily to eucharistic presence.[6] When he deals explicitly with the question of how Christ can be present in several places at once, he automatically appeals to Christ's divinity and his role as spiritual food, the two *foci* of Albert's eucharistic thought in the 1240s.[7]

Sobering as it may be to find Hugh and Albert so resolutely unimpressed by Thomas's argument, it is worth noting that neither scholar really attacks the Thomist position. They do not so much refute Aquinas as ignore him. Their approach to the problem is essentially pre-Thomist rather than anti-Thomist. The distinction is an important one, as we shall see in the next chapter.

One might assume that the Thomist view would become more widespread among Dominicans as the order rallied to his defense in the wake of the 1277 condemnations and the *Correctorium* controversy, moving rapidly from an attempt at parrying criticism to an insistence that his views be adopted by those within the order.[8] Such was undoubtedly the case, but the limited number of sources available for a history of Dominican eucharistic thought in the 1280s and 1290s makes it difficult to speak very authoritatively. Moreover, the writings of such theologians as Jacob of Metz, Durand of St. Pourçain, and John of Paris vividly demonstrate the varieties of eucharistic theology which flourished within the Dominican order at the turn of the fourteenth century.[9]

While every Dominican may not have been a Thomist on the subject of eucharistic presence, Thomas did have supporters not only inside the order but outside it as well. The Cistercian scholar Humbert of Pruilly, who seems to have lectured on the *Sentences* in Paris during the early 1290s, is described by Grabmann as a fervent supporter through whom Cistercian theology received a Thomistic stamp.[10] Such a description certainly applies to his comments on eucharistic presence, for he argues that the quantity of Christ's body is present in the manner of substance and

---

[5] See the secondary material on Albert already cited in the preceding chapter. The authenticity of this work has been questioned, but not, in my opinion, very successfully. For a bibliography regarding the controversy see Franz-Josef Necke, *Sakrament und personaler Vollzug bei Albertus Magnus,* 7.

[6] *Liber de sacramento eucharistiae,* in *Opera,* Paris, Vivès, 1899, Vol. 38, d. 3, tract. 3, c. 1, pp. 308, 311. Albert offers a number of arguments against consubstantiation, but his two favorites are derived from the words *hoc est corpus meum* and the fact that the accidents signify spiritual refreshment.

[7] Ibid., d. 3, tract 3, c. 1, pp. 313f., 376.

[8] See Frederick Roensch, *The Early Thomistic School,* for an account of this process.

[9] See Kenneth Plotnik, *Hervaeus Natalis OP and the Controversies over the Real Presence and Transubstantiation.*

[10] Martin Grabmann, "Humbertus de Prulliaco (d. 1298), O. Cist. abbatis de Prulliaco quaestio de esse et essentia," 352–69. See also Valens Heynck, "Zur Busslehre des Vitalis de Furno," 188.

that, unless the substance of bread were converted in the substance of Christ's body, Christ could be present on the altar only by a change of place, moving to the altar from his former location in heaven.[11]

By the time Humbert was lecturing at Paris and thereby sowing the seeds of Thomism among his fellow Cistercians, Giles of Rome had already accomplished the same thing within the Augustinian order. Giles taught at Paris in the later 1280s, and even at that early date Augustinian scholars were ordered to follow his lead.[12]

That lead was not entirely Thomist, to be sure. One of the most striking differences in the area of eucharistic thought stems from Giles's conviction that the form of bread could not be converted into the form of Christ's body, since the form of Christ's body is his soul.[13] Thus, in his *Theoremata de corpore Christi,* which date from the year 1276,[14] Giles argues that both the form and the matter of the bread are converted into the matter of Christ's body.[15] In this and other ways, Giles shows his independence.

Nevertheless, in the limited area which interests us at the moment, Giles is in accord with Bonaventure and Thomas. He consistently argues that the manner of Christ's eucharistic presence stems from the fact that he is present in the manner of substance as a result of the substantial conversion.[16] Moreover, he asserts that the bread cannot be annihilated, since Christ's presence in diverse places comes about through conversion.[17] Here again we find the possibilities limited to two: Either Christ becomes present through conversion of something into his body, or he must become present through change of place, leaving heaven and coming down to be present in no more than one place.

The Bonaventuran-Thomist view also seems to have made an impression on some of the more famous secular masters. Henry of Ghent is a case in point. In his ninth quodlibetal disputation, which was probably held in 1286,[18] he asks whether, by a miracle, the same body can be in several places at once. It seems that it can, he says, for it is no less possible for diverse bodies to be in the same place by a miracle, something that has actually occurred in the virgin birth and in Christ's passage through a closed door.[19] Again, the dimensions of the bread could be converted into those of Christ's body, in which case the dimensions of his body would

---

[11] Humbertus de Prulliaco, *Super sententias,* dd. 10–11, in MS Oxford, Bodl. Hatton 94, f. 115ra–rb.

[12] See the *Chartularium universitatis parisiensis,* Paris, Chatelain, 1889, II, pp. 12, 40–42.

[13] For a description of Giles's view and its repercussions, see Plotnik, *Hervaeus Natalis,* 26–30.

[14] See the bibliography cited in Ibid., 26.

[15] *Theoremata de corpore Christi,* Bologna, 1481, prop. 26, 28–30, 32–34, ff. 17r–25r.

[16] *Theoremata,* prop. 3, f. 2v; prop. 47, f. 38r.

[17] Ibid., prop. 34, f. 23v; prop. 40, f. 29v. In prop. 11, f. 7v, he asserts that eucharistic presence depends upon conversion, but he is not arguing against annihilation at this point.

[18] See J. Paulus, *Henri de Gand,* xv–xvi.

[19] *Quodl.* 9, q. 32, in *Quodlibeta,* Venice, Iacobus de Franciscis, 1613, Vol. II, pp. 128v–130r.

be on various altars. Since the dimensions can only be where the whole body is, the whole body would then be in several places at once.

Henry now argues, this time speaking for himself, that it is impossible for the same body to be in different places at the same time, for if it could be in two places it could be everywhere, which is possible for God alone. Again, a body existing *corporaliter et dimensionaliter* in several places could be hot and cold, hungry and satiated, sick and well, even dead and alive at the same time. These, he says, are more evident *inconvenientia* than the ones inherent in saying that, if a morsel of bread from the last supper had been conserved in a pyx, the body of Christ would have died on the cross but not in the pyx, since it was capable of being affected in one place but not in the other; yet the church takes the latter inconvenientia so seriously that it holds the body of Christ would have died in the pyx, although it would not have been wounded there.

If one chooses to argue that the idea of Christ being wounded on the cross but not in the pyx presents the same problems, one has failed to notice an important distinction. Christ is not in the pyx in such a way as to be capable of being wounded there, since he is not there *dimensionaliter.* Thus, he cannot be the subject of contradictory influences in the sense of being wounded in one place and not in the other. If he were present *dimensionaliter* in several places at once, such would be the case. In fact, a body which was *dimensionaliter* in several places at once would be at the same time both a single body and several bodies.

As to the comparison between a body being in several places at once and several bodies being in one place, Henry argues that the cases are not at all similar, since there is no absolute contradiction involved in the latter. The difficulty involved in the latter stems from the fact that two sets of dimensions cannot be in the same place, and such is the case, not because of the very essence of dimensions, but through something that is accidental to them.

In reply to the second argument, that the dimensions of bread could be converted into those of Christ's body and thus the dimensions of his body would be on several altars at once, Henry protests that Christ can in no way be elsewhere than in heaven except through either conversion of something else into his body or change of place. The latter would involve relinquishing his place in heaven, since it is impossible for the same body to be in different places dimensionally according to its own dimensions (*dimensionaliter secundum proprias dimensiones*), as he has just shown. Moreover, some would say that, even if dimensions were converted into dimensions, Christ still would not be present *dimensionaliter*. Instead, either the dimensions of Christ's body would inform the remaining substance of bread, or they would inform the substance of Christ's body, which would be present by concomitance. Thus the dimensions would not be there dimensionaliter, but rather through the remaining substance of bread (*ratione illius substantiae manentis*), which in turn would not be there dimensionaliter, but rather in simple and indivisible fashion, since it would be there without dimensions.

So far, Henry has been assuming a situation in which only the dimensions were converted. What if both substance and dimensions were converted at the same time? Henry argues that even in such a case the body of Christ would not be present on the altar *dimensionaliter*, for such a conversion would entail the disappearance of the eucharistic species. The body of Christ cannot be assumed to be elsewhere while remaining in heaven unless it is elsewhere sacramentally, and such sacramental presence lasts only so long as the visible species retain their identity. If body, substance, and dimensions of bread were converted into substance and dimensions of Christ's body, there would be no sacramental species and therefore no eucharistic presence.

Thus Henry agrees with Bonaventure and Aquinas in according a central place to eucharistic conversion. This is not to say that he found his predecessors' view completely satisfactory, however. Kenneth Plotnik notes a degree of concern regarding the problem of transubstantiation and annihilation and a resultant desire to tie the substances of bread and body more closely together by some rather vague statements about the bread remaining. At one point in the same quodlibetal question he affirms that "the substance of bread remains in one way, but not in another," while later in that question he says that it "remains in something, that is, in that it is now converted."[20] In a question written the following year he says that "the converted thing is something after conversion, namely that in which it is converted."[21] These efforts on Henry's part are rather tentative, and hardly add up to a further development in eucharistic thought, but they do indicate a significant area of concern which Henry shared with others in his time.

At roughly the same time, another secular master, Godfrey of Fontaines, was also considering the question of whether the same body could be in two different places without any conversion.[22] Some argue that it is possible, he says, for "whatever God can do through a medium or a middle cause he can do immediately or by his own power." Godfrey argues, on the contrary, that a thing is in place either *per se* or *per accidens*, through something else. The former involves being in the place definitively and circumscriptively. The latter occurs when something affects or is affected by something else that is in a place, or when something already existing in a place is converted into something else, as when the substance of bread is converted into Christ's body with the accidents remaining. We know from the case of Christ's presence that it is possible for a body to be in several places at once in the latter way, but multiple presence in the former way is impossible, for *per se* presence includes being comprehended by a place in such a way that nothing is outside it.

---

[20] *Quodl.* 9, q. 9, ff. 97r–98r.
[21] *Quodl.* 11, 1, q. 4, f. 194r.
[22] *Quodl.* 4, q. 5, in *Les Philosophes du Moyen Age,* tome II, Louvain and Paris, Institut Superieur de Philosophie de l'Université, 1904, pp. 250. Glorieux, *La Literature Quodlibetique,* I, 149–51, dates this *quodlibet* as 1287.

It is possible for two bodies to be in the same place, since this is not normally impeded by the very essence of dimensions, but rather by an accident, the *situs* which they normally have in a place. Through this *situs,* which is order to a place, bodies touch and hold themselves outside one another. Since it is an accident, *situs* can be removed by divine power without violating the nature of dimension. In such a case a body can penetrate another without resistance and, if the second body is in a place, the first will be in that same place *per accidens.*

The case of per se multiple presence is quite different. It would involve a self-contradiction, for the body would be commensurated with the dimensions of one place and limited to that place, yet it would also be outside that place. Godfrey makes the same point in a slightly different way by arguing that matter receives its sensible form and is determined to a place through quantity. It can receive diverse and even contrary forms in diverse parts, but it cannot receive diverse forms in the same part or be determined to different places through the same quantity, with or without conversion. The body of Christ can be in several places at once because it is locally in heaven through its own quantity and is sacramentally on diverse altars through the diverse quantities of diverse eucharistic hosts.

Godfrey goes on to emphasize that transubstantiation is necessary. Otherwise, the body of Christ could receive a new place only by changing place, leaving its former one and moving to another. He also underlines the importance of the remaining accidents. If the entire bread, substance and dimensions, were converted into the body of Christ, the bread could not be said to be present in the place where the bread had been.

Mention of the accidents and their role in determining eucharistic presence brings us to an important element in Godfrey's thought, the role he assigns to matter in separating transubstantiation from annihilation. In a long and complex quodlibetal question of 1288, Godfrey considers the question of whether God can transubstantiate a spiritual nature into a corporeal one.[23] In the process of answering, he notes that annihilation can be avoided only if something remains, and yet this must be understood in such a way that, if the whole bread, substance and accidents, were transmuted into the body of Christ, the substance of bread would still not be annihilated. In other words, one cannot point to the remaining accidents as proof that the bread was not annihilated. It is necessary that the accidents remain, not for this reason, but because through them the body of Christ is present sacramentally where the bread and wine used to be.

What else, then, can be said to remain? Clearly one must distinguish between ordinary conversion, in which there are two positive terms and a subject common to both, and transubstantiation, in which there are two positive terms and no common subject, since both form and matter are converted. Matter, then, cannot remain in any strong sense of the word.

---

[23] *Quodl.* 5, q. 1, in *Les Philosophes Belges,* tome 3, Louvain, Institut superieur de philosophie de l'université, 1914, pp. 1–6.

Godfrey rather cautiously suggests that what is transubstantiated can be said to remain inasmuch as what was converted and what it was converted into are in some way *in potentia* to one another, even though the conversion is supernatural. Even supernatural power could not effect a transformation in a case where one thing is in no way *natum* to be the other. Godfrey finds this link in matter. A rock is *in potentia* to an ass or a plant because they agree in having matter. If God should change a rock into an ass, "the rock would not be said to have been annihilated, since the whole would remain in the ass, but according to something of it, namely the essence of its matter." If an angel were produced from the rock, the latter could not be said to remain, but would be annihilated.

That this view was something more than a passing fancy on Godfrey's part can be seen in another quodlibetal question written the following year.[24] Here Godfrey repeats that the body of Christ can be locally in heaven and sacramentally on several altars because of transubstantiation, in which

the bread is not annihilated, but changes into and is in a certain way conserved in that which is truer and nobler, the body of Christ thus in a certain way containing and conserving in itself the substance of bread which is not annihilated, but is in the stated way transubstantiated into and conserved in it.[25]

Our hurried examination of the various scholars cited in this chapter, cursory though it may be, underlines two important facts. On the one hand, sensitive theologians like Giles of Rome, Henry of Ghent, and Godfrey of Fontaines recognized certain problem areas in contemporary eucharistic thought, such as the questions of whether the form of bread could be converted into Christ's soul and whether the spectre of annihilation could be avoided by positing some enduring link between the bread and Christ's body. In addressing themselves to these questions, they brought eucharistic theology beyond the state where Bonaventure and Thomas left it. On the other hand, their discussion of such problems was based upon a wide area of agreement with Bonaventure and Thomas, and this area of agreement included the notion of transubstantiation as both a sufficient and a necessary explanation of eucharistic presence.

Even as Giles, Henry, and Godfrey wrote, however, a series of theologians in a single order were attacking precisely the latter notion. It is to these theologians that we must now turn.

---

[24] *Quodl.* 6, q. 3, in Ibid., pp. 112f.

[25] Ibid., p. 113: . . . in illud quod verius est et nobilius transit et quodam modo conservatur, ipsum corpus Christi sic in se quodam modo continens et conservans substantiam panis non adnihilatam, sed dicto modo in se transsubstantiatam et conversam . . .

V. THE FRANCISCAN CRITIQUE: WILLIAM DE LA MARE, MATTHEW OF AQUASPARTA, JOHN PECHAM, PETER OLIVI, ROGER MARSTON, AND WILLIAM OF FALGAR

In the previous chapter, we saw that some Dominican theologians writing after 1256, such as Hugh of Strasbourg and Albert the Great, did not follow Bonaventure and Aquinas in making transubstantiation a sufficient and necessary explanation of eucharistic presence. Nevertheless, we must also note that Hugh and Albert did not so much reject the Bonaventuran-Thomist position as ignore it. Their discussions of eucharistic presence look backward to the period antedating Bonaventure and Aquinas. At the same time, as we have seen, other scholars inside and outside the order such as Peter of Tarentaise, Giles of Rome, Henry of Ghent, and Godfrey of Fontaines were examining and accepting the basic Bonaventuran-Thomist thesis which forms the subject of this study, even though their total eucharistic thought shows them to be more than servile imitators.

We now turn to a group of Franciscan theologians who differed from Peter, Giles, Henry, and Godfrey inasmuch as they rejected the Bonaventuran-Thomist view of transubstantiation as sufficient and necessary explanation of eucharistic presence, yet also differed from Hugh and Albert insofar as their rejection was explicit, stemming from a public examination and refutation of that view. Before doing so, however, we must make three observations. The first of these is that there were, of course, some Franciscan theologians who did not reject the view. Such is hardly surprising, given the authority enjoyed by Bonaventure and the aura of theological tidiness pervading the view itself. Thus one is quite prepared to discover that scholars like Walter of Bruges, Nicolas Ockham, Petrus de Trabibus and perhaps John of Erfurt accepted it.

Walter of Bruges, addressing himself sometime in the 1260s to the question of whether the bread is annihilated, answers that

the substance of bread neither remains nor is annihilated, but is converted into the body of Christ. The first part is clear, for when a thing is where it formerly was not, something is changed there. In this case, however, . . . Christ's body cannot be changed because it is glorified; nor can it be moved from its place, because it would then leave heaven; nor are the accidents of the bread changed, for we experience them all there; nor can the form or the matter alone be changed, the other remaining, for in that case the remaining element would be the subject of the accidents, which is false. . . . The second is clear from the role of God in the process, for, as Augustine says in his *Eighty-three Questions*, God is not the cause of a thing achieving nonbeing, and what occurs here is by God's power.[1] Thus the bread is not annihilated. It is also clear in the light of the end result, for what is changed into something better is not annihilated. It is also clear from the presence of Christ's body, which would not begin to be present here unless something were converted into it.[2]

Much later, in a *Sentence Commentary* which seems to be a product of the early 1280s,[3] Nicolas Ockham shows similar allegiance to the Bonaventuran-Thomistic view. Nicolas argues that the bread cannot remain, not only because it would then be an occasion for idolatry, but also because the body can become present only through change in itself or "a change in something else which is terminated at the body of Christ in some way."[4] Nicolas actually refers to this view as the "common position," although, as we shall see, some important people had decided to reject it even by that date.

A few years later, perhaps around 1290,[5] Petrus de Trabibus addressed the same matter in his *Sentence Commentary*. In the space of sixteen pages, Petrus announces no less than seven times that substantial conversion is the reason why Christ is present on several altars at once.[6] He rules out annihilation on the ground that,

if the bread were annihilated, it would follow that it was not converted into something else, and if the bread is not converted into Christ's body there is no way that Christ's body can be on the altar except by its own motion and descent from heaven, which is false and impossible.[7]

Elsewhere he offers the classic alternatives: A body can be where it formerly was not only through change in itself or through conversion of something into it. In the case of eucharistic presence, the former alternative would lead to a series of contradictions, such as that it would be locally in several places at once and that it would be simultaneously moving and at rest.[8]

---

[1] Augustine, *De diversis quaestionibus 83*, q. 21, PL 40, 16.

[2] *Le Questioni sull'eucaristia di Gualtiero di Bruges, O.F.M., 1225–1307*, Rome, Edizioni Francescane, 1962, 108ff.: Respondeo. Substantia panis nec hic manet, nec adnihilatur, sed in corpus Christi convertitur. Primum patet, quia ubi est aliquod, quod ibi prius non erat, ibi est aliquid mutatum; hic autem, sub speciebus, est corpus Christi quod prius ibi non erat, nec ipsum est mutatum cum sit gloriosum, nec de loco suo motum quia tunc dimisset caelum, nec accidentia panis sunt mutata quia illa sentimus ibi omnia, nec forma tantum nec materia tantum, altero manente, quia tunc alterum horum esset subiectum accidentium, quod est falsum, sed quia etiam hoc nihil faceret ad sacramenti rationem, propter quod necesse est ponere quod nihil ibi manet de substantia panis. Secundum patet tum ex parte Dei, qui ut dicit Augustinus 83 *Quaestionum*, 'non est causa tendendi in nihilum, quod autem hic fit, fit virtute Dei'; ergo panis non adnihilatur. Patet etiam ex parte termini, quia quod in melius mutatur non adnihilatur. Patet etiam ex praesentia corporis Christi, quod hic esse non coepisset nisi aliquid in ipsum conversum fuisset.

[3] See Aquilinus Emmen, "Nicolas von Ockham," 996.

[4] *In sententiarum libros quattuor commentarius*, MS. Oxford, Merton 134, f. 144vb.

[5] See Valens Heynck, "Zur Datierung der Sentenzenkommentare des Petrus Johannis Olivi und des Petrus de Trabibus," 397.

[6] MS Florence Bibl. Naz. Conv. sopp. A 5.1071, ff. 59vb–67ra.

[7] Ibid., f. 67ra.

[8] Ibid., f. 65va–vb.

The same alternatives are accepted by John of Erfurt, if Valens Heynck is correct in attributing to that author a commentary on the fourth book of the *Sentences* found in a Lüneburg manuscript.[9] Granting the probability of Heynck's attribution, we may also tentatively accept his suggestion that the work was produced somewhere between 1294 and 1304. At any rate, the author, whoever he may have been, uses the opposition of conversion versus local motion to refute both consubstantiation and annihilation and devotes an entire question to the argument that the cause of Christ's eucharistic presence must not simply be described as divine power, but rather as conversion, although divine power certainly concurs in effecting it.[10]

The second observation to be made is that Franciscan opposition to the Thomist-Bonaventuran position cannot be related *directly* to either the condemnations of 1277 or the *Correctorium* controversy. Eucharistic thought played a role in both, but in very special ways. In 1277, the orthodox understanding of transubstantiation was reflected in Tempier's condemnation of assertions regarding the inseparability of subject and accident and the impossibility of two sets of dimensions in the same place.[11] In the *Correctorium* controversy, eucharistic thought comprised one front on which the battle over the unicity or plurality of forms in man was waged, with Kilwardby,[12] Pecham,[13] Richard of Middleton,[14] William de la Mare,[15] and others[16] claiming to see sinister implications for eucharistic theology in the Thomist view, while Aquinas's adherents expressed similar doubts about the notion that there are a plurality of forms in man.[17] Clearly these were different issues than the ones we will face in the following pages. Nevertheless, having denied any direct connection, we must refrain for a while from passing judgment on whether there may be a more devious relationship.

---

[9] Heynck, "Studien zu Johannes von Erfurt," 163–96.

[10] MS Lüneburg Cod. theol. 2° 19, ff. 20rb–23ra. Thus Heynck's contention that the author was influenced by Petrus de Trabibus rather than Olivi on the subjects of grace, confession, and justification seems to be born out by the section on eucharistic presence. It is worth noting that the author's question on the cause of Christ's eucharistic presence is obviously written in opposition to the trend we shall examine in the rest of this work.

[11] *Chartularium universitatis parisiensis*, 1: 543–58; Hissette, *Enquête sur les 219 articles condamnées à Paris le 7 Mars 1277*, 287–91.

[12] See his letter to Peter of Conflans as found in the Vienna MS. edited by A. Birkenmajer, "Der Brief Robert Kilwardbys an Petrus von Conflans," *Beitrage*, 20: 60–64.

[13] *Registrum epistolarum*, London, Longman, 1885, 3: 922.

[14] *Quaestio fratris Richardi de gradu formarum*, in Roberto Zavalloni, *Richard de Mediavilla et la controverse sur la pluralité des formes*, 62–167.

[15] *Correctorium fratris Thomae*, in *Correctorium corrupterii "quare,"* Kain, Le Saulchoir, 1927, 130; *Declarationes*, Münster i. W., Aschendorff, 1956, 20.

[16] See Zavalloni, *Richard de Mediavilla*, 318.

[17] See Ibid., 260–75 and Roensch, *Early Thomistic School*, 178–225. The controversy extended well beyond the Franciscan and Dominican orders. See Giles of Rome, *In libros de physico auditu . . . eiusdem quaestio de gradibus formarum*, Venice, 1502, III, c. 1, ff. 211va–212rb (and the comments on Giles offered by Zavalloni, pp. 273–75); Henry of Ghent, *Quodl.* 9, q. 8, f. 95r; Godfrey of Fontaines, *Quodl.* 5, q. 1, p. 6.

Having said so much, we can now turn to those Franciscan theologians who comprise the real subject of this chapter. We will begin with the father of the *Correctorium* battle, William de la Mare, whose role in that battle makes him a very tempting starting-point for an examination of non-Thomist views, even though, as we have just seen, the *Correctorium* battle itself did not explicitly deal with this question.

It is not easy to place William de la Mare chronologically among the Franciscan masters at Paris. During the last few years his regency has been dated as early as 1268–69 and as late as 1274–75.[18] Given the relationships which will be suggested by the following discussion, it would be nice to anchor William more firmly in history, but precision is hardly possible at present.

Of the writings definitely attributable to William, one quodlibetal question is particularly relevant to this study.[19] In it he asks whether God can make the same thing be locally (*localiter*) in several places at once without converting anything else into it. It seems, William says, that he can do so, for the soul and accidents of Christ's body are in heaven and on several altars without anything being converted into them. Therefore God can do the same with a body. On the other hand (*contra*), if the same body can be in several places it will lead to contradictions, for if the same body is locally present in Paris and Rome it might be plunged into fire in Rome while sitting on ice in Paris, or it might be moving in Paris while sitting quietly in Rome. Thus it would be hot and cold, moving and unmoving, all at the same time.

Now William has cleared the way for his own view. It is to be held by all the faithful, he says, that Christ's body is simultaneously present in several places at once. Why it is such remains a matter for dispute, however. Some say it occurs because the body is united with divinity, but such cannot be the case, for by the same token it could be everywhere. Others say it is due to the conversion of bread and wine into Christ's body, but this argument too seems questionable, for it is hard to see how such conversion could make the body of Christ be present anywhere except where it already was before the conversion. Since all of the bread is converted into Christ's body, none at all remaining, it is hard to see how

---

[18] Gerard Etzkorn and Ignatius Brady, *Fr. Rogeri Marston O.F.M. Quodlibeta Quatuor*, Quaracchi, College of St. Bonaventure, 1968, Prolegomena, p. 14*, say 1268–69. J. P. Muller, "Wilhelm de la Mare," 1138, says 1274–75, following Glorieux, *La Literature Quodlibetique*, 117 and Franz Pelster, "Einige erganzende Angaben zum Leben und zu den Schriften des Wilhelm de la Mare OFM," 75–80. Ironically enough, Glorieux, one of those who pioneered the 1274–75 dating, later opted for a date earlier than 1270, while Ignatius Brady has suggested recently that William must have been master regent after Pecham and therefore after 1270. See Glorieux, "Sermons universitaires parisiens de 1267–68," 51–58; idem, "Maitres franciscains régents à Paris," 324–32; Brady, "Questions at Paris, c. 1260–1270," 688f.

[19] Glorieux, *La literature quodlibetique*, 2: 117, lists the question as *Quodl.* I, q. 3, but notes the lack of any formal indication that these questions are actually *quodlibeta*. He lists several manuscripts, including Vat. Borgh. 361, f. 147vb–148rb; Florence Bibl. Laur. Plut. 17 sin. cod 7, f. 15rb–va; and Bibl. Laur. Plut. 17 sin. cod. 8, f. 165ra–va.

the conversion could be the reason why Christ's body begins to be present where the bread once was. On the contrary, one might rather argue that, through the conversion, the bread begins to be present in heaven in the place of the body, instead of the body becoming present on the altar in the place of the bread. Thus, William concludes, "I believe that such [conversion] is not necessary, but only God's will and omnipotence, and that what God does with Christ's body he can do with any other, with or without conversion."[20] Hugh of St. Victor seems to hold this position when he says God could do otherwise if he wished.[21]

William must now deal with the opposing argument. Of the properties of the body, he says, some are absolute and some relative. "Hot" and "cold" are absolute, and thus if they belong to a body in one place they will belong to it in other places as well. If it is cold in Paris, it will be such in Rome as well. William does not linger over this point, and he tends to speak in absolutes—*either* hot *or* cold—as if he expected one or the other to win, but one might assume that he would see the Parisian ice and Roman fire as moderating one another's effect, thereby producing a single body temperature for both locations. Unfortunately, he does not explicitly say so.

The case is quite different with movement and rest, which are relative properties. They inform the body only in relation to a place. Thus they need not be uniform if a body is in several places. In fact, we see that Christ's body is moved with the host at one altar while remaining quiescent at another.

Another work is highly relevant to the problem of eucharistic presence, but its attribution to William is questionable. I refer to the commentary on the third and fourth books of the *Sentences* found in two manuscripts, Florence Bibl. Nat. A 2.727 and Toulouse 252.[22] Franz Pelster argues in favor of William de la Mare as author of this commentary,[23] while Ferdinand Doucet feels that Pelster's arguments are at best weak.[24] The issue is unsettled, and must await a more thorough treatment than it has been accorded so far; yet William's authorship remains a very live possibility and it is certainly worthwhile to examine the work at this point.

The *Sentence* commentary in question offers a treatment of eucharistic presence which is neither very long nor, on the whole, very original. In the Toulouse manuscript, there are nine pages of questions on the eucharist,

---

[20] Vat. Borgh. 361, f. 148ra: Propterea credo quod illa non est necessario ratio sed sola voluntas et omnipotentia dei et quod facit deus de corpore Christi in conversione panis potest facere absque omni conversione et quod facit deus de corpore Christi potest facere de corpore alio et per conversione alicuius in ipsum et sine conversione. I follow the reading of MS. Florence, Bibl. Laur. Plut. 17, sin. cod. 7, which differs only slightly from Plut. 17, sin. cod. 8. Vat. Borgh. 361 omits a good deal of the passage, obviously a scribal error.

[21] William quotes *De sacramentis*, liber 3, pars 8, c. 11, in *PL* 176, p. 469: Qui corpus fecit, locum fecit . . . et quando vult aliter fecit.

[22] Florence, Bibl. Nat. A 2.727, ff. 165r–193v; Toulouse 252, ff. 127r–158v.

[23] F. Pelster, "Les 'Declarations' et les questions de Guillaume de la Mare," 405f.

[24] V. Doucet, "Quaestiones centum ad scholam franciscanam," 194f.

of which five deal with eucharistic presence and conversion. Time after time the author avoids extensive treatment of a problem by simply referring the reader to Bonaventure, on whom he is highly dependent.

Nevertheless, some interesting things are said about the relationship between eucharistic presence and conversion, particularly in a passage dealing with the objection that Christ cannot be present in the eucharist because nothing which has limits (*terminos*) can be contained outside those limits.[25] The body of Christ is present as in a place, the author says, where it is present through the mediation of the dimensions of quantity (*mediantibus dimensionibus quantitatis*) and its dimensions are commensurated with those of the place. The body of Christ is only in one place, heaven, in this way, "and thus it is not outside the limits of its place in the manner in which it is in place by its own dimensions, but only through the dimensions of the bread which was converted into the body of Christ." Thus it is not present on the altar as in a place but rather as in a sacrament containing and signifying, by the power of conversion (*ex vi conversionis facte*), and this way is possible.

One might expect the author to end his discussion at this point, but he does not. "Another explanation (*ratio*)," he goes on to say, "is assigned by Hugh." The present order of things exists, not because there is any inherent reason for it (*non quia convenit talis ordo*), but because God wishes it (*quia deus vult*). Thus God has determined that, according to the course of nature, one body is in one place only; yet by God's will that same body could be in several places.[26] Thus one should say that the body of Christ, although it is in diverse places, is not outside its limits, for when a body is in several places its limits are also in several places.

Here the author seems to have gone a long way toward refuting the notion that Christ's sacramental presence demands substantial conversion. He has not gone all the way, however, as a later passage shows. In this passage he is arguing that the bread is not annihilated. Every change (*motus*), he says, is named by its *terminus ad quem*. The eucharistic conversion is terminated at the body of Christ, and thus it cannot be called annihilation, for it is impossible to explain how Christ's body begins to be present except by positing either some change (*motum vel mutationem*) in his body or in something else.[27] Here we seem to encounter an unconditional acceptance of the alternatives assumed by the Bonaventuran-Thomist position.

Can the two passages in the *Sentence* commentary be harmonized? Perhaps they can. One can say that, in the first passage, the author merely argues that there is nothing contradictory about a body being present in several places at once. In the second passage, he is concerned with the

---

[25] Toulouse 252, f. 153vb.

[26] Here again we are dealing with Hugh's *De Sacramentis,* which the author quotes verbatim.

[27] Toulouse 252, f. 155va: Alias non posset poni quomodo corpus Christi inciperet ibi esse nisi per motum vel mutationem propriam aut alterius terminatam ad ipsam aliquo modo.

question of how Christ *comes to be* present in the sacrament. Here he concludes that Christ's presence must be realized through conversion because only in this way can some change in Christ himself be avoided. The argument is a reminder that eucharistic conversion may be deemed necessary, not only because presence *per modum substantiae* seems to offer a way of avoiding the contradictions apparently entailed by multiple presence, but also because conversion of something into Christ seems to offer a way to avoid the apparent alternative, change in Christ himself. Normally, of course, the two problems are combined. Change in Christ can be seen as entailing the wrong sort of presence. For example, presence on several altars through local motion would involve contradictory motions and, ultimately, multiple presence *ut in loco*. In this work, however, the two issues seem to be dealt with separately.

Granting that the passages might be harmonized through such a distinction, we must still ask whether that distinction was seen by the author himself or whether the preceding paragraph must be viewed as a desperate attempt on my part to extricate the author from a problem which he himself failed to recognize. Much as I would like to endorse the former alternative, the author's treatment of these questions is too skimpy to afford a definite answer. Note, however, that if this *Sentence* commentary is by William de la Mare it would probably antedate his quodlibetal question. Thus, if he is the author, he eventually rejected the necessity of conversion as suggested in the passage regarding annihilation, partly because of considerations concerning divine omnipotence already present in the *Sentence* commentary, but also because of his later conclusion that eucharistic conversion was in any case an inadequate explanation of Christ's eucharistic presence.

It is worth observing at this point that a situation similar to the one seen in William de la Mare's commentary on the *Sentences* can be found in the works of another Franciscan of roughly the same vintage, Matthew of Aquasparta. Matthew must have been a *sententiarius* at Paris in the early 1270s and a regent master there around the middle of the decade. In 1279 he went to Rome as lector at the papal court.[28]

In a quodlibetal question apparently written in Rome around 1279 or 1280, Matthew asks whether the substance of bread can be converted into the substance of Christ's body.[29] On the one hand, he says, God's ability to effect such a conversion is well attested by authority, including Matthew 26:26, Ambrose, Augustine, Eusebius, and Hugh of St. Victor. On the other, it is confirmed by reason. God's omnipotence extends to all those

---

[28] Victorinus Doucet's introduction to the *Quaestiones disputatae de gratia,* Quaracchi, College of St. Bonaventure, 1935, xvi–xxiv, says he was a bachelor of the *Sentences* at Paris in 1271–72 and a regent master in 1277–78.

[29] Matthaeus de Aquasparta, *Quaestiones disputatae de incarnatione et de lapsu aliaeque selectae de Christo et de eucharistia,* 202–205. The editors, p. 6*, place this question during Matthew's years as lector at the papal court, 1279–87. Glorieux, *La litterature quodlibetique,* 195, dates it 1279–80.

things that do not imply a contradiction. Thus he can convert one substance into another whenever he wishes. In fact, Matthew adds, he actually does so.

> For according to the faith we suppose that the body of Christ is present where it formerly was not. If, however, there is no transmutation into the substance of bread, the body of Christ must necessarily be there through transmutation in itself. Thus it is there through creation, generation, or change of place. It clearly is not present through creation or generation. If it is present through change of place, it descends from heaven, and thus, since it is on the altar, it does not remain in heaven, or else one and the same body will be in two different places, which cannot be. If, therefore, the body of Christ is not there through change in itself, then it must be present through change in the substance of bread. This change can only be conversion and transition.[30]

Matthew goes on to say that this conversion resembles creation insofar as nothing remains common to both terms, yet it differs from creation and resembles generation insofar as the *terminus a quo* is an existing thing. To an objection that the body of Christ would necessarily receive existence through such a conversion, he replies that it receives, not existence, but presence.[31]

In another quodlibetal question, however, Matthew explicitly asks whether God can make the same body be locally present in several places at once.[32] His solution is unambiguous: "Whatever others may have said, I say without prejudice that God through his omnipotence can make one body be in many places locally." He distinguishes between that which is considered impossible because it exceeds the power of a created being and that which is impossible because it involves an inherent contradiction. Multiple local presence, like the virgin birth, belongs in the former category, while two plus three equaling four belongs in the latter. Matthew crowns his argument by quoting the standard passage from Hugh of St. Victor.

Here again, we find a theologian arguing, on the one hand, that Christ must be present through conversion, and, on the other hand, that a body can be locally present in two different places at once. Here again one is tempted to harmonize the passages by suggesting that the author sees the necessity of transubstantiation as dictated by the need to avoid, not multiple local presence, but change in Christ's body. Unfortunately, such a neat

---

[30] *Quaestiones disputatae de incarnatione et de lapsu*, pp. 204f.: Quod autem ita sit, manifestum est. Supponimus enim corpus Christi secundum fidem ibi esse, ubi prius non erat. Si autem nulla fit transmutatio in substantia panis, tunc oportet quod ibi sit per transmutationem factam in ipso. Aut igitur est ibi per creationem, aut per generationem, aut per loci mutationem. Non per creationem aut generationem, hoc manifestum est. Si per loci mutationem, ergo descendit de caelo; ergo cum fit in altari, non remanet in caelo; aut unum et idem corpus localiter erit in duobus locis, quod esse non potest. Si igitur non est ibi corpus Christi per mutationem factam in ipso, ergo per mutationem factam in substantia panis. Haec mutatio non potest nisi conversio et transitio.

[31] Ibid., p. 205: . . . non fit ut sit quod non erat, sed fit ut illud quod erat, sit ubi non erat.

[32] *Quodl.* IV, q. 1, MSS. Assisi, Bibl. Comm. 134, f. 151ra–rb; Todi 44, f. 213v–214r.

solution is ruled out by the fact that the quodlibetal question on conversion
explicitly eschews both. Thus there is no way of avoiding the conclusion
that the passages cannot be reconciled. Matthew either experienced a
change of heart or he had not thought the matter through clearly.[33]

However the Parisian careers of William de la Mare and Matthew of
Aquasparta should be dated, they probably overlapped with that of another
major theologian, John Pecham. Pecham was an extremely influential figure
whose teaching career extended from Paris to Oxford and to the papal
court, and whose later activities as archbishop of Canterbury form a major
chapter in the history of English Aristotelianism and its critics.[34] For our
purposes, it is sufficient to note that Pecham was at Paris throughout the
1260s and was regent master from 1269/70 to 1271/72.[35]

The most important place to look for Pecham's views on eucharistic
presence is in his *Questions on the Eucharist*.[36] Although there is no way
of dating this work with certainty, a notation in the only surviving manuscript says, "These are the questions disputed and determined by brother
John Pecham at Paris."[37] If this information can be trusted, the *Questions
on the Eucharist* must have been produced between 1269/70 and 1271/
72, since they were probably written after Pecham attained the *magisterium*.
Thus we are blessed with a first-rate source for his eucharistic thought at
the moment when he made the transition to recognized scholarly maturity.

---

[33] One is reminded of Efrem Bettoni's comment that "Matthew is a master who feels at
ease only when he finds himself in good company and moves on the solid ground of common
opinion. He becomes irresolute and evasive as soon as one asks him to express a personal
view on some question regarding which even those of his school are divided. One has the
distinct impression of finding oneself before a man who takes refuge from speculative ad-
ventures as much as possible, preferring to leave in the shadow that which divides and hold
to that which unites; a man, in short, who, on the plane of ideas as in life, had the temperament
not of a warrior but of a diplomat." "Matteo d'Aquasparta e il suo posto nella scolastica
post-tomistica," 246. Nevertheless, it is impossible to say how aware Matthew was of the
problem he faced at this point, or how conscious he was of the varying ways in which his
fellow Franciscans were beginning to solve it.

The discerning reader may recognize that I have omitted mention of another work by
Matthew, his commentary on the *Sentences*. This work is extant in a single manuscript, Assisi
132, which is in Matthew's own hand. Practically illegible in itself, it is totally unreadable
in the microfilm copy currently at my disposal, and I would have to spend a great deal of
time with the actual document in order to make sense of it. Thus I have elected to eliminate
it from consideration. I might note, however, that at f. 275rb Matthew does quote the standard
passage from Hugh of St. Victor, although not in the standard context.

[34] For the latter topic see Decima Douie, *Archbishop Pecham*, Oxford, Clarendon Press,
1952, Ch. VII. For Pecham's relations with Aquinas see Ignatius Brady, "John Pecham and
the Background of Aquinas' *De aeternitate mundi*," 2: 141–78.

[35] See Douie, Archbishop Pecham, pp. 5–9; Ignatius Brady, "Questions at Paris, c. 1260–
1270," 688f.; Conrad Harkins, "The Authorship of a Commentary on the Franciscan Rule
published among the Works of St. Bonaventure," 192.

[36] *Quaestiones de eucharistia*, MS. Florence Bibl. Naz. J 1.3, ff. 7rb–18vb. For the contents
of this manuscript see H. Spettmann's prolegomena to his edition of *Johannis Pechami Quaestiones tractantes de anima*, Münster i. W., Aschendorff, 1918, as well as F. Tocco's introduction
to Pecham's *Tractatus contra Fr. Robertum Kilwardby*, in *Fratris Johannis Pecham . . . tractatus
tres de paupertate*, Aberdoniae, Typis Academicis, 1910, 99–108.

[37] Bibl. Naz. J 1.3, f. 19va.

Having opted for the authenticity of one source, we must now note that another one is clearly inauthentic. Here again we are dealing with a single manuscript, Oxford Bodley 859, which contains a series of questions twice identified, albeit in another hand, as by Pecham.[38] In one case, the questions are referred to as "Pecham on the fourth [book] of the Sentences." Although this ascription has been taken seriously by at least one competent historian,[39] it is now generally recognized that the questions cannot be attributed to Pecham.[40]

We are now ready to examine the *Questions on the Eucharist*. The first question is whether the nature and whole substance of Christ's body is in the sacrament of the altar.[41] Pecham's treatment of this matter is intriguing, but less so than what is to come and we can safely pass over it to the next question, in which he considers whether the body is *dimensionatum* in the eucharist and whether these dimensions are commensurated with those of the bread. He refutes the view of an anonymous "some" that the same matter serves as subject of the form and accidents of bread and of the form of Christ's body, as well as the view that the bread is converted into the body of Christ without its accidents. The flesh of Christ, he says, is neither perfect nor perfectable without organic existence. Moreover, although the intellect can abstract quantity from a quantified substance, such as the three angles from a triangle, a substance cannot exist in its perfection without dimension, just as a triangle cannot really exist without three angles.[42] He goes on to offer the familiar explanation that, where substance is present *mediantibus dimensionibus*, it "follows the manner of dimensions," with part being present in part. Where quantity is present *mediante substantia*, however, it is present in the manner of substance, which, insofar as it is substance, "needs neither a great nor a small place, since it abstracts from any *ratio* of this type."[43] In a later response to one objection, Pecham acknowledges that God could, through his omnipotence, make the body of Christ exist without an accident of this kind *de potentia absoluta*. Such an existence would, however, be imperfect and therefore detract from the dignity of the sacrament as well as its significance. Moreover, the *ratio sacramenti* requires that the body be *organicum*, and it cannot be such unless it is also *quantum*.[44]

At this point Pecham seems to have answered both questions, but he

---

[38] Bodl. 859, f. 332r.

[39] H. Spettman, "Pechams Kommentar zum vierten Buch der Sentenzen," 64–74, which lists the contents of the manuscript.

[40] See, for example, F. Pelster's review of Spettman's article in *Scholastik* 3 (1928): 447. Pelster asserts that the questions "gehören vielmehr sämtlich dem grossen Komplex an, die der Grundlage für die Summa des Alexander von Hales bildete," a claim which he pursues in other articles, such as "Die Quaestionen des Alexander von Hales," 401–22, 501–20.

[41] Bibl. Naz. J 1.3, ff. 8rb–9vb.

[42] Ibid.

[43] Ibid., f. 10vb. See also 11ra–rb.

[44] Ibid., f. 11ra. At f. 14rb, he says that God could make a substance without any absolute accidents, but not without any relative accidents.

has only answered the first, that of whether the body has dimensions. He now proceeds to ask whether these dimensions are commensurated with those of the bread, and answers that they are not. There are, he says, three predicaments involved in commensuration: quantity, *ubi* and *positio.* *Ubi* follows upon quantity, for it is nothing other than circumscription of the body proceeding from circumscription of the place. *Positio* follows upon quantity through the mediation of *ubi.* No secondary cause acts without the influence of the primary cause. Thus, if the first cause is removed, all effects of the second cause will also cease. In this case, although quantity is present, the normal effect does not follow, because God does not allow it to act. Later, however, Pecham grants that *positio* and *dimensio* are present through concomitance.

In the process of dealing with the question of whether Christ's body is present in every part of the host, Pecham fields the objection that, if such were the case, his body would be there *confuse,* with the hand and foot occupying the same place. He replies that such would be true only if one part was *situaliter simul* with another. While it is true that the hand is where the foot is, confusion does not result, for, just as many rays of the sun are together through reflection *situaliter et inconfuse,* so the many parts of Christ's body are together not *situaliter* but *presentialiter,* and are thus ordered to one another, but not in respect to quantity. Hence others say that the parts are ordered to the whole but not to the place.[45] Elsewhere he says the extremes of Christ's body are distant from one another through comparison of the parts with one another, but not through comparison of the parts with the place.[46]

Like others before him, Pecham raises the question of whether Christ is in each part of the host before it is broken. He attacks the mirror analogy because it contains errors in itself—for example, it is incorrect to say that multiplication of the images is caused by breaking the mirror, since such would not occur if all the parts remained where they were—and because it fails to recognize that Christ is present through the words of institution and therefore cannot begin to be present in any different way long after those words have been spoken.[47] Nevertheless, he later hazards a guess that the whole is converted into the whole rather than the parts into the parts.[48]

So far, Pecham has favored the notion of presence *modo substantiae* as an explanatory principle. He now shifts his ground slightly and argues that Christ is present in each part of the host, not only because he is there *modo substantiae,* but also because of the *dos subtilitatis* enjoyed by a glorified body. The former explains why each part of Christ's body is commensurated with every part of the host. The latter explains how each

---

[45] Ibid., 12va.
[46] Ibid., f. 11rb.
[47] Ibid., ff. 11vb–12ra.
[48] Ibid., f. 12va.

part of the body can penetrate and be under each part of the bread.[49] Thus Pecham employs an old, honored notion in a new and limited context.

As to the matter of subsistent accidents, Pecham asserts that the first cause can directly produce the effects of a second cause in any case where no contradiction is entailed. Thus God can separate accidents from substance and accidents from accidents in most cases, yet he cannot produce alteration, augmentation, or color without quantity. Quantity is, in fact, the principle accident inasmuch as it is the one most immediate to substance, and therefore all other accidents are in substance through the mediation of quantity.[50] Pecham counters the charge that *inesse* is part of the very definition of an accident by protesting that such *inesse* must belong to an accident in aptitude but not necessarily in actuality. Here again he is in general agreement with Bonaventure and Thomas.

Turning to the nature of eucharistic conversion, Pecham explicitly asks whether Christ's body could be present in the eucharist without some substance being converted into it. He cites a series of arguments for the affirmative position. For example, the presence of Christ's body is the effect of some uncreated cause, and whatever an uncreated cause can achieve by means of a created cause it can effect without that cause. Again, the same *per se* cause makes the body become present in the eucharist and conserves it there. If God can conserve the body in the eucharist without the substance of bread, he can also effect its presence without conversion of the bread. Again, if God can make two bodies exist in the same place without conversion, why can he not make the same body exist in two places without it? Again, if Christ's body ceases to be present in the eucharist without change in itself, why can it not become present without anything changing into it? Again, if a body which can be created in heaven and on earth is already in heaven, there is no reason why God cannot also make it be present on earth through creation or in some other way. Finally, it is more repugnant to the nature of Christ's body to be present through transubstantiation than without it, for the body does not take on being in the conversion but simply begins to be present in a new place. Thus transubstantiation does not really solve the difficulties inherent in Christ's eucharistic presence—the enigma of how a body can become present in a distant place without change in itself is just as pressing whether one posits transubstantiation or not—but rather adds a few problems of its own, such as how one can avoid talk of annihilation and speak of conversion when there is no common subject.[51]

These arguments are followed by another brief for the necessity of transubstantiation. A passage from John of Damascus seems to suggest that conversion and local motion are the only two ways in which Christ can be present. Again, the acquisition of something new requires some

---

[49] Ibid., f. 12rb.
[50] Ibid., f. 13vb.
[51] Ibid., f. 14va–vb. I have omitted two inconsequential arguments.

change. Thus, if Christ comes to be present in the eucharist, this must involve change in Christ or in something else. A series of other arguments follow, most of them pointing to the conclusion that presence without conversion would entail change in Christ.[52]

Having presented both sides of the argument, Pecham notes that, although the truth of the matter is unclear, it is less dangerous to attribute to divine power what cannot be done because of some repugnance on the part of created being than to deny God's power to do something which is actually possible. Thus Pecham concludes "without prejudice, that by divine power the body can be present without either conversion or local motion." This conclusion follows from consideration of the way in which Christ begins to be present, remains present, and ceases to be present in the eucharist. It follows from the first, for whatever God can do with the aid of secondary causes he can do without them; from the second, because Christ is conserved in the eucharist through divine power alone; and from the third, because Christ ceases to be present without any motion and therefore can become present in the same way. This view seems to be supported by Hugh of St. Victor's comment that he who made one body of Christ be in one place did as he wished, and if he had wished to do otherwise he could have. Nevertheless, God has chosen to produce eucharistic present through conversion for the greater comfort of the faithful, since this way makes it easier for us to grasp Christ's presence. Again, through the containing species we are led to awareness of the thing contained.[53]

In response to the quotation from Damascene, Pecham suggests that it does not present all the ways in which Christ can become present, but only those which are more fitted to our intellects. As to the problem of *mutatio,* he concedes that there is such, but only in a weakened sense. There is properly change of place when a thing moves from place to place, less properly so when the thing is present in a new place and yet the first place is not abandoned.

Pecham also asks whether, granting transubstantiation, God could make Christ be present locally both in heaven and on earth. Here again he offers a full set of arguments for each position. Those who take the affirmative view can argue that, just as substance is converted into substance, dimension can be changed into dimension. If such were to occur, however, dimension would exist according to the manner of dimension and therefore be locally present. Again, Christ appeared after the ascension without descending from heaven and thus was locally present in two places.[54]

The first two arguments cited for the other view involve anomalies in the matter of size. It is argued that multiple local presence would involve a contradiction, inasmuch as a thing in a place is precisely equal to that place, and thus a thing locally present in two places would be equal to

[52] Ibid., ff. 14vb–15ra.
[53] Ibid., ff. 15vb–16ra. See Hugh of St. Victor, *De sacramentis,* liber 3, p. 8, c. 11.
[54] Ibid., f. 15ra. Two more rather inconsequential arguments follow.

an area double its own size. Again, if a thing can be in two places at once, it can be in all places, and thus something a foot long will be equal in size to the whole world.

Another series of anomalies arise from the very notion of what it means to be an individual. For example, every individual is "here and now," and thus an individual cannot be "here" in several places at once any more than he can be in several times at once. Again, an individual is divided from other things, yet multiple local presence would entail being divided from oneself. Finally, there is an anomaly concerning the finitude of an individual. Every finite being has its own limits (*terminos*) and, if it were outside those limits, it would be infinite.[55]

Having presented the arguments, Pecham notes that "wise men contradict wise men" on this question. The issue is whether such presence would involve a contradiction. If one feels that it does, one can reply to the first argument for multiple presence that, if dimension should be changed into dimension, then the *locus*, an accident following the dimension of the bread, would be lacking. Thus, if the dimensions of bread were converted into those of Christ's body, his body would still have only one *locus*.[56] In other words, it would still only be in heaven. Pecham also offers a possible reply to the argument concerning Christ's appearances after the ascension, but it is not entirely clear.[57]

If one wishes to take the opposing view and defend the possibility of multiple local presence, one can reply to the first argument concerning size that a thing locally present in two places would not be equal in size to both places combined, any more than such would be the case if the thing were present in two places successively. The proper answer to the second argument concerning size is that God can make a thing be present in one place naturally and another supernaturally, but he cannot make it be present in all places, since such presence is not possible for a creature.

The two arguments regarding individuality are quickly disposed of. The first one would be valid only if something had more than one *hic* naturally, whereas in this case it would occur supernaturally. The second is invalid, for nothing is divided from itself unless one part is separated from another.

To the argument that multiple local presence would entail being outside one's own limits, one can reply that the body would not be outside its own intrinsic limits, but only outside extrinsic limits dictated by a given place.[58]

Pecham touches upon the problem of multiple local presence in one other work, his Roman *quodlibet*,[59] which was presumably written between 1276 and 1279. There, having explicitly asked whether the same man can

[55] Ibid., f. 15ra.

[56] Ibid., f. 16ra.

[57] Ibid., f. 16ra: Ad secundum, quod corpus Christi vere apparuit, vere de celo descendit ut in hoc preiudicium est sanctis superne civitatis quia tali elongatione ab eis ascendi non potest.

[58] Ibid., f. 16rb.

[59] *Quodlibet Romanum*, Rome, Spicelegium Pontificii Athenaei Antoniani, 1938, q. 10.

be in several places, he alludes to the case of Saint Ambrose, who was reported to have appeared at the tomb of Saint Martin without leaving Milan. In the *contra* section, Pecham cites the argument that such multiple presence would violate the principle that an individual thing is undivided from itself and divided from others.

In his response, Pecham considers it unlikely that Ambrose was physically present in Martin's tomb. He prefers to think in terms of an ecstatic vision on the part of the observers or a successful performance by some clever angelic impersonator. "Some say," he reports,

that just as God makes his body, which is only in one place locally, be in many places sacramentally, thus he could, if he wished, make that same body be in several places locally through total conversion of the bread, substance and accidents into his body, and, if he can do so with his own body, he can do so with any other. I do not believe, however, that this was done with Ambrose.

One might be tempted to read these remarks as a negative answer to the entire question,[60] but Pecham really denies only the statement concerning Ambrose. The question itself is left wide open, just as in his *Questions on the Eucharist.*

While William de la Mare and John Pecham were gaining scholarly recognition in Paris, another Franciscan of more ambiguous reputation was studying there. Although it is impossible to say precisely when Peter John Olivi's stay in Paris began or ended, we can gather from his own testimony that he was present at the general chapter meeting of 1266 and attended Bonaventure's *Collations on the seven gifts of the Holy Spirit* in 1268.[61] Olivi left before attaining the magisterium[62] and was a lector in southern France in time to be censured by Jerome of Ascoli, who was minister general of the order from 1274 to 1277.[63]

If Olivi's Paris education dates from the 1260s and his teaching career from the 1270s, his extant writings on the eucharist may date from no earlier than the 1280s. Valens Heynck argues that his most sustained treatment of the subject, a treatise on the sacraments, was written after 1283 and probably after 1285.[64] Although Heynck's view has much to recommend it,[65] any serious attempt at dating must depend upon a more exhaustive study of Olivi's unpublished works than has been attempted to date.

Having alluded to Olivi's treatise on the sacraments, we might as well begin our analysis at that point. Olivi asks in the treatise "whether Christ

---

[60] Ferdinand Delorme, in his introduction to the *Quodlibet Romanum,* p. XL, does precisely that.

[61] *Epistola ad R.,* in *Quodlibeta,* Venice, 1509, f. 51 (63) 2; *Queastiones de perfectione evangelica,* q. 16, M.S. Rome, Vat. lat. 4986, f. 71rb; *Tractatus de usu paupere,* M.S. Rome, Vat. lat. 4986, f. 56r; *Lectura super apocalypsim,* M.S. Rome, Bibl. Ang. 382, f. 69ra. The first citation documents Olivi's presence at the *Collationes,* the last two his presence at the chapter meeting.

[62] *Epistola ad R.,* in *Quodlibeta,* Venice, 1509, f. 51(61)v.

[63] See David Burr, "The Persecution of Peter Olivi," 35f.

[64] Heynck, "Zur Datierung einiger Schriften des Petrus Johannis Olivi," 349.

[65] See my own comments in Burr, "Olivi and Baptismal Grace," 5–7.

can simultaneously be in all places or accidents which are (or can be) converted and can be present in such a way as to be entirely in every part." He replies that such "is an infallible and indubitable truth of the Catholic faith for which we ought to be ready to die."[66] An impressively thorough discussion of the matter follows. In the course of that discussion Olivi finds himself announcing that, while no one doubts God's role as first cause, there are different opinions regarding the immediate cause of Christ's presence.[67] Some say that Christ is in the species by the very fact that God converts the bread into Christ's body. Thus some say that God could not give the body this mode of being except through conversion of another being into it.

Others say that, when God creates a body and simultaneously gives it a *locus,* creation and the provision of a *locus* are not the same thing, since in that same creation God could have put the thing in some other place. In the same way, conversion and provision of a locus must be distinguished. God could convert the bread into the body of Christ existing in heaven. Moreover he could give Christ presence in the eucharistic species without conversion, just as He can give a thing a new *locus* without creation.

"Which of these views is truer," Olivi says, "I leave to my God," yet he cannot resist adding that the second one seems more likely to him. In the first place, if presence is intrinsically tied to the conversion, is it tied to the conversion as taking place or as having taken place? If the former, then Christ's presence might be expected to cease as soon as the process of conversion is completed. If the second, then it is hard to see how his presence actually does cease with the destruction of the species.

Again, conversion really involves (*ponit*) nothing except the body of Christ. Thus, if one ties presence in the species with conversion, one would have to identify Christ's body with its presence in the species, which is obviously incorrect.

Again, Christ's eucharistic presence is either identical with the conversion or diverse from it. The former cannot be, and in the latter case one can argue that conversion is the effective cause of the presence only by involving oneself in many absurdities.

Again, the conversion is related to the remaining accidents of the bread only *per accidens,* and thus through conversion Christ is no more in these particular accidents than in any others. If one should reply that any action operating on a thing existing in a given place is in that place, this is not always true, but, even if it were, then it would follow that the body of Christ would thereby gain a special relationship, not to the eucharistic accidents, but to the place where the bread was when the conversion took place. Thus, when the accidents were moved, the body of Christ would not move with them, which is patently false.

Again, even if one assumes that eucharistic presence can occur only

---

[66] Vat. lat 4986 (hereafter L), f, 146v; Vat. Borgh. 13 (hereafter B), f. 26va.
[67] B. f. 28rb; L, f. 149v.

through conversion, it is still possible to argue that God could effect conversion in such a way that Christ would be present in a divisible manner. Just as God could convert each part of the bread into the whole Christ, he could also convert a mass of bread the size of Christ's body into that body in such a way that each part of the former became a part of the latter. In this way, through conversion, the body of Christ would not be in each part of the accidents. Olivi assures the reader that he has not advanced this argument in order to suggest that God could not effect such a conversion, but only as a warning to those who assume that the difficulties of local presence are somehow automatically erased by linking eucharistic presence to transubstantiation.

It should be noted at this point that Olivi prefers to think of eucharistic presence, or any presence for that matter, as a *relatio* or *respectus.* When he inquires concerning the *quidditas* of Christ's existence in the eucharist, he replies that it is not the substance of Christ's body but rather "a certain related being."[68] The *respectus* of eucharistic presence is a different type of *respectus* than that by which a body is ordinarily related to a place. In eucharistic presence, "the substance of Christ's body is related in the manner of presence (*respicit praesentialiter*) to the essence of the species taken absolutely, not involving their *situatio* or *locus* or the position of accidental parts, but only the real being (*realem emptitatem*)."[69]

In searching for examples of *respectus* of presence which do not involve local presence, Olivi mentions those of the soul to the body, a body or corporeal place to an angel who is present to that body or place, and created being to God creating and conserving that being. There are, he says, other examples, but not of the same type. For example, there is the relationship of simultaneity which binds two bodies existing at the same time, and there are the relationships of similitude, identity, equality, etc.[70] Elsewhere he offers what he himself describes as a weak example, the central point in a circle, which is present to all lines of a circle and to the entire surface and depth immediately surrounding it.[71]

Olivi foresees the objection that such a *respectus* cannot be placed within the confines of Aristotle's predicaments. He replies that it is one thing to deny it a place in some predicament created by God, and quite another to say that it is not in a predicament assigned by Aristotle, except among those who take Aristotle for God and accept his views as infallible. Perhaps one should say that it is a certain species of a more general predicament which can be called *assistere vel insistere vel esse in alio.* If Aristotle did not see things that way, so much the worse for him. He also failed to

[68] L, f. 149r, B, f. 28rv.
[69] L, f. 146v; B, f. 26va.
[70] L, f. 146v–147r; B, f. 26va. See also L, f. 150v and B, f. 29va, where he appeals to similarity in color as analogous.
[71] L, f. 150 r; B, f. 28vr.

provide adequate room for conversion of bread into the body of Christ, creation, being created, and the union of the divine and human in Christ.[72]

Thus eucharistic presence is a type of *respectus* which can be added to or removed from the body of Christ. Olivi denies that its addition or removal would necessitate any change in Christ other than the purely accidental addition or subtraction of a *respectus*,[73] but he is open to several explanations of what would happen if God annihilated the species, leaving the mode of being in Christ. On the one hand, it might be argued that one of the extremes cannot be annihilated without annihilating the mode of being as well, and thus the mode of presentiality would disappear with the disappearance of the species. On the other hand, it could be suggested that the mode of being will remain according to that which it posits in the subject, but will not remain as actually joined to the other term of the relationship. Olivi cites the example of a hand clutching an apple. The apple could be destroyed, leaving the hand in the same position but without the pressure of the apple. A third theory might be proposed, according to which the eucharistic presence is a *relatio habitualis* which does not necessarily include the actual existence of the other term, just as is the case with the knowledge by which we know many things which do not actually exist.[74]

Olivi's view of presence as a *habitus* does not prevent him from accepting the distinction between that which is present through the conversion and that which is present through concomitance. In the species of wine, only the blood is present *ex se*, while the body is there concomitantly, since it is naturally united to the blood.

Olivi distinguishes between presence *concomitative*, which is based upon natural unity with the converted body and by which something is really present under the species, and presence *per accidens*, which "posits nothing real." In explaining the latter Olivi cites those things which are extrinsically related to Christ's body as it exists in heaven, such as the clothes it might be wearing or the fact that there may be saints embracing it and kissing it. Such things should be said to be present in the eucharist only *per accidens*. He offers the example of color being seen per se, while the subject of color is seen concomitantly and the other accidents of the same subject like taste, odor, etc. are not said to be seen except *per accidens*.[75]

Anyone familiar with the Thomist use of the color analogy[76] may note that Olivi has given it a peculiar twist. The distinction between Thomas and Olivi becomes more obvious as he turns to the question of whether quantity is present only by concomitance. Some scholars, he notes, would say it is present only in this manner, and that it is impossible for it to be

---

[72] L, 151v; B, f. 30rb–va. The theme is a favorite one with Olivi.
[73] L, f. 151v; B, f. 30rb.
[74] L, 150r–v; B, f. 29ra–rb.
[75] L, f. 147v; B, f. 27ra.
[76] *Summa theologiae*, III, q. 76, a. 5 ad 1.

there in any other way. More often, some of these scholars seem to say that it is present only *per accidens*. They argue that nothing is there *primo* and *per se* except that into which the substance is converted, and that the quantity of Christ's body could not be present *per se* except in such a way as to be commensurated and coextended with the parts of the *locus*. They claim that Christ's mode of existence in the eucharist is not physical or mathematical but rather metaphysical, since the substance is not there as it is informed by natural accidents or as it is *quanta* and the subject of quantity, but only *secundum puram rationem substantiae*. In no other way, they say, could Christ be entirely in each part of the eucharistic species.

Olivi suggests that, unless he is mistaken, these scholars say things that are superfluous, unintelligible, false and impossible. They also say things that are unusual and dangerous to the faith. Finally, they offer uncertain theories as if they were substantial elements of the Christian faith.

They say superfluous things because it can be demonstrated that the essence and parts of any quantity can be present to each part of the species just as easily as it can be shown that the substantial parts can be so present. Although quantity is *situalis* in itself, it has many types of presence which are not such. For example, it is not *situalis* as it is present to God creating and conserving it. Again, it has a relationship of temporal simultaneity with other things.

Olivi's opponents say unintelligible things in suggesting that there is a mode of being which is neither physical nor mathematical, but merely metaphysical. Metaphysicians, Olivi objects, do not consider things according to the proper *rationes* of their species, but only according to the common *ratio* of being. Thus one would have to say that Christ was not in the species insofar as he was a human body or even a body, but only insofar as he was a substance.[77]

They also speak unintelligibly in asserting that the whole body of Christ is simultaneously in each part of the species because it is simple and its parts are simplified through abstraction from its quantity. "Who," Olivi asks, "can understand that statement?" They are equally unintelligible when they say that the quantity of Christ's body is really present, but only according as it has the *ratio* of a simple and indivisible thing by being founded in substance.

These scholars say things which are false and impossible, for a human body cannot be abstracted from quantity and still retain its substantial integrity, nor can it attain, through abstraction, a simplicity or simultaneity of parts which would allow it to be entirely in each part of a quantified body. Again, what they say is false because there is no *ratio* of substance in the human body except as extended in parts, for each part of the body has its own proper and partial *ratio* of substance different from the parts.

Other objections follow. Olivi observes, for example, that if the body

---

[77] L, 27v; B, f. 147vb.

is there *secundum rationem substantiae* and as it is abstracted from all quantity, it is there without any *ratio* of time or duration and thus cannot be said to be present now or to have been present yesterday. Moreover, it cannot be said to be present with a certain number of parts, with two eyes, with two feet, etc.

Olivi's opponents say things which are dangerous to the Christian faith. They affirm that God cannot convert the bread or accidents of bread into the quantity and accidents of another body or into that body according as it is *quantum;* yet there is no reason for making such an affirmation. Again, they are saying that God cannot make the quantity of Christ's body be present in each part of the species; yet such an argument provides occasion for saying the same thing regarding the body of Christ itself. Again, they are arguing in essence that God cannot make the body of Christ be present according as it is an organic and human body. Olivi notes that none of these affirmations can be defended by appeal to the authority of the canons of faith or the *sancti.*

His opponents say uncertain things as if they were certainties. For example, they say that the quantity of substance does not differ from the quantity of the accidents, and that quantity adds something really diverse from the substance or accidents which are thus quantified. Olivi observes that he has dealt elsewhere with the possibility of doubting such assertions.[78]

Against whom is Olivi actually arguing? One's first reaction would be to say that he is refuting an essentially Bonaventuran-Thomist position, but a closer look will indicate that such is not entirely the case. Thomas, Bonaventure and others would say that quantity is present through concomitance, but they would not affirm that the body of Christ is present as abstracted from its quantity. In fact, Bonaventure explicitly rejects such a possibility. Thomas Aquinas does say that the dimensive quantity of the body is present *concomitanter et quasi per accidens,* but he has not drawn the sort of distinction Olivi favors between presence through concomitance and presence *per accidens,* and thus his use of the term *per accidens* does not have the same significance given it by Olivi.

Nevertheless, despite any uncertainties involved, Olivi obviously does have trouble with the essentially Bonaventuran-Thomist formulation. Such is the case partly because he rejects the notion of quantity as an entity distinct from the subject in which it inheres and favors the notion that "quantity means nothing other than the parts of quantified things extrinsically related to one another with *situs* and *positio.*"[79] Thus when one speaks of the quantity of Christ's body, one does not refer to something which can be added or subtracted like a particular color or a pleasant

---

[78] L, 149r; B, f. 28ra.
[79] *Quodlibeta,* f. 49v. Olivi never asserts this position, but he clearly favors it. See Burr, "Quantity and Eucharistic Presence: The Debate from Olivi through Ockham," 5–44, or Idem, "The Persecution of Peter Olivi," 55–61.

odor, but one refers rather to the fact that the parts of the substance are arranged in a certain way. When quantity is seen in this light, it follows that not only substances but accidents have their own quantity (i.e. their own parts spacially related to one another).

Once quantity is pictured in this way, the distinction between presence *ex vi conversionis* and presence through real concomitance becomes a good deal less useful than Thomas would have imagined. One can still make the distinction, speaking of the body as present under the species of bread *ex vi conversionis*, while the blood, soul and accidents are present through real concomitance, i.e. because they are really and indissolubly joined with the body in heaven. Nevertheless, a little reflection will show that the distinction no longer explains why a normally extended body is completely present in each part of the species. Christ's quantity cannot be present through concomitance in the sense that his blood or his color can, for his quantity is not an entity separate from his substance as the blood and color are. Thus one cannot invoke the notions of conversion and concomitance in order to show why Christ's quantity is present on the altar and yet he is not related to a place there as he is in heaven. To put it another way, the Olivian view of quantity gravely compromises any attempt to explain eucharistic presence by saying that, through substantial conversion, Christ's quantity is present *modo substantiae*.

This point can be made more effectively by turning to another important source for Olivi's eucharistic thought, one that can be dated a bit more accurately. I refer to his polemic against a fellow scholar whom Olivi describes elsewhere as "Brother Ar"[80] and who may or may not be identified with Olivi's fellow Franciscan Arnold Galhardi. This polemic, which was probably written in 1280 or 1281,[81] ends with an appendix of sorts in which Olivi defends his view of quantity, which was already drawing heavy fire[82] and would eventually be censured by the Paris commission which examined Olivi's works in 1283.[83] Here Olivi proceeds in good scholastic fashion. He relates objections to his view, presents arguments in favor of the view, then refutes the objections. In order to streamline

---

[80] Letter to R, *Quodl.*, f. 52(64)r. See Burr, "The Persecution of Peter Olivi," for a discussion of Brother Ar's identity.

[81] See Joseph Koch, "Die Verurteilung Olivis auf dem Konzil von Vienne und ihre Vorgeschichte," 489–522, and my comments on Koch's work in "The Persecution of Peter Olivi," pp. 37–40. The work in question, which I shall hereafter cite as *Polemic*, is published in *Quodl.*, ff. 42r–53r.

[82] According to *Polemic*, f. 49v, his opponent had described the view as "ridiculous and dangerous." Olivi insists that he merely recited it without assertion. In his letter to R, *Quodl.*, f. 52(64)v, Olivi includes the view among those which he is charged with maintaining, but still insists that he "simply recited it in order to consider more deeply the subtleties of metaphysical principles."

[83] See the *Littera septem sigillarum*, in *Archivum Franciscanum Historicum*, 47 (1954), 52, which simply censures that statement that "the predicaments are not really distinct," and the *Responsio P. Ioannis ad aliqua dicta per quosdam magistros parisienses de suis questionibus excerpta*, in *Archivum Franciscanum Historicum*, 27 (1935), 405, which explicitly refers to quantity.

the discussion a bit, we will examine the objections and his response to them, then look at his positive arguments.[84]

Of the seventeen objections considered by Olivi, two are related to eucharistic presence. One argues that, if Olivi's view of quantity were accepted, it would follow that in the eucharistic conversion the quantity of the bread would be converted into the body of Christ. If such were the case, the remaining accidents would not have quantity and would not be subjected in anything, since, according to the masters, quantity is the only subject of the eucharistic species and of the transmutations undergone by them up to the time of their destruction. Moreover, since quantity is commonly considered to be an accident, this view would imply that an accident is converted into the body of Christ.

The other objection seems to reverse the one just presented, arguing that, according to Olivi's view, the quantity of Christ's body would be present through conversion rather than through concomitance. Thus the body could not be entirely in every part of the host. In fact, it could not be present at all if, as some say, Christ can be present in the eucharist only because he is there *per se* and directly according as he is substance rather than according as he is quantified, since substance as substance does not involve *situs* (*substantia inquantum substantia non determinat sibi situm*).

It is easy to see that these objections misrepresent Olivi's position to some extent. In the former one, for example, there is no recognition of the fact that, according to Olivi, the accidents have their own quantity, since they have their own parts spatially related to one another.

The problem is not one of sheer misinterpretation, however. In effect, the latter objection argues that Olivi's view could not be correct because, if it were, eucharistic presence would be impossible. Here we have a clear recognition that the Olivian view of quantity makes the Thomist-Bonaventuran approach to eucharistic presence quite untenable. In fact, the objection more or less presupposes the sorts of limitations Thomas Aquinas would place on multiple presence.

Olivi recognizes this fact, and his rebuttal strikes directly at those limitations. He notes that any view according to which God cannot convert something into the quantity of Christ's body or into that body insofar as it is quantified, or any view according to which God cannot make the whole quantity of Christ's body be present in each part of the host through conversion, "does not seem safe and, in fact, I believe it to be heretical."

A strong reaction, but it is easy to see why Olivi considers it to be in order. Of course God must be able to convert something into the quantity of Christ's body, for, if he could not do so, then eucharistic presence would be impossible. Given Olivi's view of quantity, "converting the bread into the quantity of Christ's body" simply means "converting the bread into

---

[84] The objections are found at f. 50r, the responses at f. 51v–52v.

Christ's body, which has part existing outside of part in a particular pattern." Whatever Bonaventure and Thomas might have said about Olivi's view of quantity, they would have agreed that Christ's body must be so arranged in order to be a living body.

Having castigated the opposing view as a threat to divine omnipotence, Olivi goes on to suggest that it is also sheer nonsense. What do these people mean, he asks, when they say that the body of Christ "is present according as it is a substance, but not according as it is quantified except perhaps *per accidens*"? If, he says, they mean that "the body is not there in a local and dimensional manner, so that the various parts of it are arranged in different ways in relation to the various parts of the *locus*," then their statement is basically correct but very improper and misleading. If, however, they mean to suggest that "the *ratio* of quantity is not present according as it is quantity, but only according as it is being, then this view is not only insecure but unintelligible, since the *ratio* through which it is being is not really separate from that through which it is quantity." Again, when they say that the body of Christ is present according as it is a substance, but not according as it is quantified except *per accidens*,

do they mean by this statement that the parts of the body are not present according as they are situated in a continuum outside one another, but are rather present, as it were, within one another and all together, constituting, as it were, one simple body? They had better not think that! I ask, then, what they do intend to say, for I have no clear understanding of it.[85]

Olivi offers twenty-five arguments in favor of his own view. These tend to be phrased in the form of assaults on the opposite view, and three of them are directly relevant to eucharistic theology. The seventeenth argument asserts that, if all the accidents in the sacrament were extended by a single accident of quantity as the opposing view apparently assumes, then it would seem to follow that God could not separate them in such a way that the parts of each accident were continuous and ordered to one another as they were before. Who, Olivi rhetorically asks, would dare to say that God could not do such a thing?

According to the eighteenth argument, it follows from the opposing view that the body of Christ is not in each part of the host or even in the host at all by virtue of the eucharistic conversion (*ex vi conversionis*), for if the substance of bread insofar as it is abstracted from all *situs, positio, continuatio* or *extensio* is converted into Christ's body, there is no reason why the body should be in one place rather than in another through this conversion. In short, the sort of substantial conversion envisaged by Olivi's opponents is a conversion abstracted from relationship to any particular

---

[85] *Quodlibeta*, f. 52r. "Nunquid per hoc intendunt quod partes corporis non sint ibi secundum quod sunt in corpore extra se invicem situate et sibi invicem continuate, sed potius quod ibi sint quasi intra se invicem ut omnes simul coexistentes, et quasi unum simplex corpus constituentes? Absit hoc sentire. Quero igitur quid per hoc intendunt quia non clare intelligo."

place. Here one suspects that the argument may tell less heavily against the opposing view of quantity than Olivi would care to admit, since, as we have seen, his treatise on the sacraments robustly attacks the notion that presence is intrinsically tied to conversion in any case.

The nineteenth argument claims as a consequence of the opposing opinion that God could not make the quantity of Christ's body be present in the eucharist *per se* and directly as the substance is. Thus He could not convert the bread into the quantity of Christ's body. "A Catholic," Olivi warns, "should be careful in deciding whether it is safe to say such a thing, for it seems to me to be very dangerous and to detract greatly from God's power and perhaps from the sacrament of the altar." Here again, Olivi's appeal to divine omnipotence is more than an evocation of unrealized possibility. Given Olivi's idea of quantity, the quantity of Christ's body must be directly present as the substance is, if the substance of Christ's living body is to be present at all.

We have seen that this little treatise on quantity forms an appendix, as it were, to Olivi's polemic. The eucharistic implications of the quantity issue are also explored in the body of the polemic, where Olivi portrays his adversary as asserting that God can make the body of Christ exist alive and yet unquantified. This view, Olivi observes, is against the common opinion. He cites Bonaventure to the effect that, although a substance can exist without quantity, it cannot so exist and still be living and organic. Olivi goes on to argue that a being which exists entirely in a single point and is thus indivisible cannot be organic because, in order to be such, a being must have situatio of organs and organic parts. In the case of Christ's body, can one imagine it alive and functioning without the heart, head, and other principle members being related to one another in the necessary way? How, for example, would the sensitive powers operate in such a being? Again, would such a body be simple in the sense that a point is simple or in the sense that an intellectual being is simple? The former is ruled out by a whole series of considerations, not least of which is the fact that a point belongs in the genus of quantity. Thus we are left with the latter, in which case Christ's body would not be a body at all, but rather a spiritual being.

We might parenthetically note that Olivi also tries to portray the opposing view as dangerous because it leads to a sacramental version of the docetic heresy. The church, he says, has condemned those who held that man will rise again in *corpore aereo* and those who claimed that Christ came in a celestial body rather than one composed of the elements. Both groups were heretical because they denied the reality (*veritatem*) of the human body, one in the final resurrection and the other in the incarnation. The view under discussion does the same thing, for if the body can exist in a single point and still remain a real body, it necessarily follows that all the things which cannot be present in this form are accidental to it. Olivi cites Christ's invitation to his disciples to verify the reality of his resurrected body by touching it. This invitation presupposes that a real body has density, something lacking in a point.

In the treatise on the sacraments, Olivi argues against the views of an anonymous group simply labeled "others." In the polemic, his opponents are less anonymous. We know that he is chiefly attacking a "Brother Ar," a fellow Franciscan and probably a fellow native of southern France. We may even be able to guess intelligently that "Brother Ar" was really Arnold Galhardi. Having said so much, we must add that it does not help one bit in characterizing the position Olivi attacks. Here, as in the treatise on the sacraments, one often senses that the position assaulted by Olivi is not precisely the one held by either Bonaventure or Thomas, but one is hard pressed to decide whether the difference lies in Olivi's opponent or in the peculiar twist he himself gives to the opposing view. It is interesting that, on several occasions in the polemic, Olivi explicitly notes that his antagonist is following Thomas Aquinas. Unfortunately, no such comment occurs in the section on quantity and eucharistic presence.

One other aspect of Olivi's eucharistic thought might be mentioned. Here we must take a final glance at the treatise on the sacraments. In a question on whether the bread can be converted into the body of Christ, Olivi cites an argument against this assertion according to which such cannot be the case because there both would and would not be annihilation of the bread. There will be annihilation because that thing of which nothing essentially remains, either in itself or in another thing, is truly nothing and therefore has been annihilated. Nothing of the bread remains, and therefore it is annihilated. On the other hand, there would not be annihilation because annihilation is not conversion of being into being, but rather into pure nonbeing.[86] To this argument, Olivi replies that

The bread is not annihilated taking annihilation simply and properly, according to which, that is, a pre-existent being is terminated in nothing in every way, because the being and the essence of bread are not terminated in nothing but rather in the essence of Christ's body. The major of the aforesaid argument is, however, false, or at least must be subjected to a distinction, as is also the case with the minor. The idea that something of a thing remains can be interpreted in two ways. Either it remains under the *ratio* of the prior essence or in another essence through the conversion of one into the other. If we think of it as remaining in the first way, the major premise is false, because not everything which does not so remain in its prior essence is annihilated. If "to remain" is taken in the second sense, then the minor premise is false.[87]

---

[86] L, f. 140r; B, f. 17ra.

[87] Ibid., L, 142v; B, 20vr: Ad secundum dicendum quod panis non est adnihilatus sumendo adnihilationem simpliciter et proprie secundum quam scilicet esse praexistens secundum omnem modum terminatur in nihil, quia esse et essentia panis non est terminata in nihil sed potius in essentiam corporis christi. Maior autem praedictae rationis vel est falsa vel est distinguenda et idem est de minora, remanere enim aliquid de aliquo potest intelligi dupliciter, aut sic scilicet quod sub ratione prioris essentiae maneat aut sic quod (B: quia) in alia essentia maneat per hoc scilicet quod (B: quia) prior essentia eius facta est illa alia. Si igitur remanere sumatur primo modo tunc minor est falsa.

The opening qualification is intriguing and encourages one to look for some sense in which the bread may perhaps be annihilated, but Olivi does not oblige us. In the long run, he simply subscribes to the accepted view that the bread is not annihilated because it is converted. In the ensuing argument, which involves a long and tortuous examination of the way things and events succeed one another in the eucharist, he always distinguishes rather clearly between conversion and annihilation.[88]

We will now turn to Franciscan scholar Roger Marston, who probably knew Olivi at Paris. Marston was a student there in 1270 and presumably for a time before that date. His chronology is the subject of some dispute, but there is much to be said for the hypothesis that he returned to England around 1272 with John Pecham, who had been his master in Paris and continued to be such at Oxford. His education continued at Oxford throughout the 1270s, with a one- or two-year interruption while he taught at Cambridge, and ended with his inception during the school year 1281–82.[89]

Our source for Roger's eucharistic thought is the series of quodlibetal questions composed by him around 1282–1284. These questions provide us with only a partial view of his position, but it is enough to demonstrate that here, as in many other cases, Marston is heavily dependent upon his master. The close relationship between the two scholars has been recognized for some time, although its precise degree has been disputed, with Decima Douie asserting that Marston's veneration for Pecham "caused him to carry plagiarism to lengths unusual even in the middle ages,"[90] while the editors of Marston's quodlibetal questions are gentler in their assessment.[91]

Pecham's mark is certainly visible in the questions dealing with eucharistic presence, although, as the editors remark, Marston contributes some material of his own. He agrees with his predecessors that Christ is impassible in the eucharist because his quantity is there *mediante substantia* and therefore in the manner of substance, rather than substance being present *mediante quantitate* and thus being dimensively or locally present.[92] He also agrees that, although Christ cannot be present in a quantitative manner or *per modum quantitatis*, he must be present with his own dimensions or he could not have a perfect existence there.[93] Nor does Marston have any quarrel with the notion that Christ is present through the eucharistic conversion.[94]

He follows Pecham, not only in those areas where Pecham is consistent with the more or less Thomist understanding of eucharistic presence, but

---

[88] Ibid., L, f. 144r, B, f. 23ra; L, f. 144r, B, f. 23rb; L, f. 145r, B, f. 24vb.

[89] This chronology is proposed by Etzkorn and Brady in the *prolegomena* to *Fr. Rogeri Marston O.F.M. Quodlibeta quatuor*, Quaracchi, College of St. Bonaventure, 1968, 9*–31*, after a careful examination of the evidence and a critique of alternate solutions.

[90] *Archbishop Pecham*, p. 13.

[91] *Quodlibeta quatuor*, pp. 69f.

[92] *Quodl.* II, q. 7, pp. 163f.; *Quodl,* II, q. 9, p. 180; *Quodl.* III, q. 23, pp. 357f.

[93] *Quodl.* III, q. 24, p. 358.

[94] *Quodl.* II, q. 9, p. 179.

also in assertions which diverge sharply from that view. For instance, Marston agrees with Pecham in simply attributing the presence of Christ's soul to divine power rather than to real concomitance through its insep- arable union with the body.[95] More to the point, Marston deals with the question of whether the same body can be locally present in several places at once, and his answer is nothing more than an abbreviated form of Pecham's in his *Questions on the Eucharist.* Like Pecham, he notes that "wise men contradict wise men," then goes on to show how either view might be defended.[96] Thus he agrees with Pecham in seeing it as an open question.

This is not to say, however, that Marston does nothing more than restate for the 1280s the views formulated over a decade earlier by his master, Pecham. In a question on whether quantity and substance are the same, Marston rejects the essentially Olivian view.[97] He does so by advancing a notion of indeterminate dimensions which includes a good deal of what Olivi meant by quantity. For Marston, these indeterminate dimensions, far from being identical with quantity, actually precede it because they are prior to the introduction of substantial form in matter, whereas all accidents are caused by the existence of form in matter. The point is, of course, a minor one for our investigation, but it does show how different questions were perceived as new and exciting in the 1280s.

Another scholar of roughly the same Parisian vintage, Guilelmus Petrus de Falgar, takes a more resolute stand in a pair of quodlibetal questions presumably dating from his regency in the early 1280s.[98] William asks whether God can make a body in Paris become present in Rome without passing through intermediate places.[99] He first argues the affirmative po- sition on the ground that God can do *per se* whatever he does by means of a creature. Since he performs the act in question through transubstan- tiation, he can do it without transubstantiation. If conversion were nec- essary, it would be such because it was the cause of that presence; yet it cannot be the formal cause, since the body of Christ remains present after transubstantiation has taken place. It cannot be the final cause, for the body of Christ performs that function. It cannot be the material cause because, if such were the case, the body of Christ would not remain present once the conversion had been completed. Finally, it cannot be the efficient cause, which is divine power.

The preceding argument is introduced, not with the words *videtur quod sic,* but with the words *arguo quod sic.* Nevertheless, a brief contra section

[95] *Quodl.* II, q. 8, pp. 169–71. Pecham, *Quaestiones de eucharistia,* MS Florence Bibl. Naz J 1.3, f. 15vb, explicitly rejects the idea of presence through inseparable union, whereas Marston ignores it, one of several ways in which Marston diverges from Pecham in the course of the question.

[96] *Quodl.* III, q. 4, pp. 320–22. Compare Pecham, *Quaestiones de eucharistia,* ff. 15ra–16rb.

[97] *Quodl.* II, q. 29, pp. 291–94.

[98] See Glorieux, *Litterature quodlibetique,* II, p. 125.

[99] MSS. Brugges 185, f. 2ra–va; Paris, Bibl. Nat. lat 14305, f. 154rb–vb.

is then offered, based on a supposed parallel between movement through time and movement through space. Since transition from one time to another implies movement through intervening points of time, transition from one place to another must involve passage through intervening places. In short, the alternative to conversion is a trip through all the towns between Paris and Rome.

William now arrives at his *respondeo* section. There is, he says, a difference of opinion on the matter. One group of theologians who base their views on "the laws of bodies and places" say God cannot make a body be in two places at once without conversion of something else into that body. The very idea involves a contradiction, since circumscriptive presence implies that no part of the located thing (*locatum*) is outside the limits of the place (*locum*).

In order to understand this matter, William says, two things are necessary, purgation of the soul and illumination of the understanding. An extended comment on each is offered, with ample reference to Augustine and Gregory the Great, before William finally comes to the point relevant to this study: We know that God makes the body of Christ become present through conversion without passing through intermediate points. What God does by means of a creature he can do *per se*. William cites the standard passage from Hugh of St. Victor and alludes to the case of St. Martin and St. Ambrose, which he accepts as valid evidence. To the argument of those obsessed with the "laws of bodies and places" he replies that a thing cannot be simultaneously present in two places by its own power, but we know by the light of faith that it can be so by divine power, "hence this and similar things are better believed than understood, or rather we do not understand them nor are we able to do so unless we first believe." The objection based on a similarity between time and place is countered by denying that similarity. Time is a *mensura communis transiens*, while place is a *mensura determinata permanens*.

Note that the question is relevant to the question of multiple presence, although not originally aimed at that problem. Later, in the course of another question, William explicitly states that a body can be in several places because, if God can effect such multiple presence through transubstantiation, he can do so without it.[100]

---

[100] Brugges 185, f. 12va. I have not had the opportunity to compare the text of Paris, Bibl. Nat. lat. 14305.

VI. THE FRANCISCAN CRITIQUE: RICHARD OF MIDDLETON, VITALIS DE FURNO, AND WILLIAM OF WARE

When some of Olivi's writings were submitted to a commission of Parisian scholars for judgment in 1282, one member of that commission was a young bachelor of theology named Richard of Middleton. Olivi's eucharistic thought was not directly implicated in that episode, but it was indirectly involved in a way that is of some interest for our study of Richard. Olivi's view of quantity was attacked by the commission,[1] and we know from other sources that the objection to that view was based partly on what many scholars considered its sinister implications for eucharistic presence. Richard of Middleton attacks the Olivian view of quantity in both his *Sentence* commentary and a quodlibetal question, and in the latter he evokes eucharistic dogma.[2] Nevertheless, in other ways Richard agreed with Olivi's eucharistic thought, and the area of eucharistic conversion offers one such point of agreement. Here again we are dealing with both Richard's *Sentence* commentary and his *quodlibeta*.

Although our knowledge concerning the normal course of theological education would encourage us to consider the *Sentence* commentary to be earlier than the *quodlibeta*, the matter is probably a bit more complicated in Richard's case. Hocedez argues persuasively that Richard was a *sententiarius* at Paris in 1278–79 and 1779–80 but revised his commentary at a later date. The fourth book cannot have been finished before the end of 1294, although it is earlier than 1298.[3] Nevertheless, despite the fact that some sections of the *Sentence* commentary stem from a period well after the *quodlibeta*, we will consider it first here.

In his *Sentence* commentary, Richard asks whether Christ is in the eucharist according to his real quantity and answers that he is, because quantity is conjoined with substance. Substance is there *per se* or *immediate*, while quantity is there *per concomitantiam*. Thus it is not commensurated with the quantity of the species so that part is commensurated with part.[4] Richard acknowledges that God could make the substance be present without any accidents whatsoever. Nevertheless, it would not be fitting

[1] See Burr, "The Persecution of Peter Olivi," 54–61.
[2] *Commentum super quarto sententiarum*, Venice Dionysius Bertochus, 1489, IV, d. 12, a. 1, q. 1; *Quodlibeta*, Brescia, 1591, *Quodl.* II, a. 2, q. 2. He was not alone. Another voice from the 1280s, Raymond Rigaldi, offers the same theological argument. See his *Quodlibet* IV, MS. Todi 98, f. 18vb.
[3] Edgar Hocedez, *Richard de Middleton*, 49–75.
[4] IV *Sent*, d. 10, a. 1, q. 2.

in this case, since Christ's body could not be separated from all accidents and remain living.[5]

Having granted that the body of Christ is not present through quantity and therefore is not there as *in loco*, Richard goes on to inquire whether God could nevertheless make his body be in the species as *in loco*. Some theologians, he observes, say that God could do so without allowing the body to be circumscribed by the species, for He can preserve a cause while inhibiting the action of that cause. Other scholars think this view irrational, since, for a body to be *in loco*, it must not only be contained but also commensurated and configured with the place.[6] Thus Christ is in only one place, heaven, as *in loco*, but is in several other places through substance.

Richard himself feels that it is within the realm of divine possibility for Christ to be locally present in several places at once. It seems equally impossible for two bodies to be in the same place, and the philosophers deny that such can be; yet God actually did make a glorified body exist in the same place as an unglorified one. Again, God could transmute the dimensions of the bread into the dimensions of his body just as he converts one substance into the other. Again, God could convert various parts of air, each the size of Christ's body, into his body. Again, God can do without secondary causes what He does with them. Transubstantiation is the efficient cause of Christ's presence in the eucharist, and thus, by acting without the efficient cause, God could effect eucharistic presence without transubstantiation.[7]

Richard then argues that God could transmute the substance of the bread into the quantity of Christ's body.[8] He also considers, without rejecting it, the possibility that God could transmute the same substance of bread into several bodies.[9]

Richard believes, of course, that Christ is entirely in each part of the host. It does not follow from that fact that Christ is in an infinite number of parts, for, although a continuum can be divided endlessly, the parts of a continuum do not have actual distinction. In response to the perennial objection that the various parts of Christ's body must be present in a disorderly and confused manner, Richard simply notes that they are distinct and ordered to the whole body, but not in relation to the containing species.[10]

When Richard later turns to the subject of eucharistic conversion, he begins on familiar ground, reviewing alternatives considered by Innocent III. According to Innocent, some say that the bread and wine are converted because the body and blood of Christ begin to exist under the same accidents in place of the bread and wine, just as a grammarian says that "a" is

---

[5] Ibid., Ad. 3.
[6] Ibid., a. 2, q. 1.
[7] Ibid., a. 2, q. 2.
[8] Ibid., a. 3, q. 1.
[9] Ibid., q. 2.
[10] Ibid., a. 6, q. 1.

changed into "e" when a tense change occurs. Against this view, some would argue that the body of Christ is present without change (*mutatio*), which would be impossible without conversion of something into it. Others say that the substance of bread actually remains, while the body of Christ becomes present under the species through divine power. Against this opinion, some would advance the same argument as in the previous case.[11]

Richard now abandons the role of impartial reporter and takes his own stand. The contrary argument, he suggests, would not be terribly convincing to one holding either opinion. Such a person would undoubtedly reply that a body which begins to exist in a new place without ceasing to be present in the old one is not changed (*mutatus*) on that account, except perhaps in the sense of being in a new place, which would be the case even if conversion were posited.

No, Richard says, the aforesaid opinions must be combatted in other ways. The canon of the mass, speaking of the bread, says *fiat corpus*. Again, Christ says *hoc est corpus meum*, not *hic est corpus meum*. Again, if the bread and wine remained, the priest would break his fast by partaking and thus could not take the sacrament twice in one day.

These arguments are worth pondering. Richard begins by positing an argument which would militate against both consubstantiation and a "weak" view of eucharistic conversion in which the bread is said to be converted into the body of Christ simply because one succeeds the other. He then cites what he obviously considers to be a cogent objection to that argument and offers three substitute arguments in its place. Of the three substitute arguments, two are clearly aimed only at consubstantiation, while the third, the fact that the canon of the mass says *fiat corpus*, hardly represents a powerful refutation of the "weak" notion of conversion.

Nevertheless, Richard's interest in the matter does not seem to be aroused, and he moves on to other questions. Shortly thereafter, when he encounters the traditional question of whether the bread is annihilated in the conversion, he treats it in cursory fashion, announcing that the bread is not annihilated because it is converted into the body of Christ.[12]

Richard's position is clarified, not only by his *Sentence* commentary, but also by his first two *quodlibeta*, which are considered to have been composed around Easter and Christmas, 1285.[13] In the first of these, having raised the question of whether God can make a body exist in several places at once,[14] he outlines the negative view, presenting the same argument already given in his *Sentence* commentary and commenting that its defenders think of it as *per se notum*. As in the *Sentence* commentary, Richard

---

[11] Ibid., d. 11, a. 1. q. 1. See Innocent III, *De sacro altaris mysterio libri sex,* cap. 20, in PL 217, col. 870.

[12] Ibid., a. 1, q. 3.

[13] Roberto Zavalloni, *Richard de Mediavilla et la controverse sur la pluralité des formes,* 507; Hocedez, *Richard de Middleton,* 49 and 478f.

[14] *Quodl.* I, q. 2.

opts for the opposite view, which "seems safer because it is further from error, because it is consonant with authority, and because it can be shown to be true through the truth of the sacrament of the altar." It is further from error because, by holding it, one removes oneself further from the error of those infidels who say Christ cannot be on several altars at once. Richard turns his view into a general axiom: "When, however, there are two opinions, one of which is further from a pernicious error than the other, the error is to be avoided through that opinion which is more remote from it, if that opinion can be substantiated or sustained."[15]

As to authority, the opinion is perfectly consonant with the words of Hugh of St. Victor. It is also consonant with the power of the sacrament, Richard says, for it is certain that Christ's body is on several altars. To be sure, he is there only by mediation of the species, and the dimensions of his body are present only by mediation of its substance. Nevertheless, it remains true that the same corporeal substance is in separate things according to place (*in rebus separatis secundum locum*). If a substance can be noncircumscriptively under various species in different places, it can be noncircumscriptively in various places. If God can make it be present noncircumscriptively in several places, he can make it be so present circumscriptively or locally.

Should one object that Christ is present to the various species through transubstantiation, it is true that such is the case, but the point is not a terribly relevant one, for transubstantiation cannot be the reason why Christ remains present. Thus the formal reason for his existence under the species cannot be transubstantiation but rather "some relation of the substance directly to the species" (*aliqua relatio ipsius substantiae immediate ad ipsas species*). Transubstantiation is merely the efficient cause of Christ's presence, and whatever God does by means of an efficient cause He can do without it. Thus, if God can make Christ be present through conversion, it follows that He can effect the same presence without conversion.

Richard notes that, just as it seems in our imagination (*imaginabiliter*) to be contrary to the laws of body and place that one body should be in several places at once, so it seems equally impossible that two bodies should be in the same place. In fact, all the philosophers do consider the latter to be impossible. Nevertheless, we see that God does the latter with both glorified and unglorified bodies, and thus it seems probable that he can also do the former.[16] Multiple presence may be *contra imaginationem*, but it is not *contra rationem*. In reply to the argument that multiple local presence would involve "being here" and "not being here" at the same time, Richard notes that "being here" does not necessarily include "not

---

[15] Ibid.: Quando autem sunt duae opiniones, quarum una est magis remota ab uno pernitioso errore, quam alia, magis declinandum est per illam, quae magis remota est ab errore, si potest ratione talis substentari, vel sustineri.

[16] For Richard's view of the reason why two bodies cannot be in the same place see *Quodl.* II, q. 15.

being there." To the argument that a finite creature, by its very nature, can be in only one place at a time, Richard replies that such creaturely limitations simply mean a thing can only be present in one place at a time through its own power (*per virtutem propriam*).

The idea that eucharistic presence logically demands transubstantiation is also implicitly denied in another question dealing with the possibility of local movement in an instant.[17] Richard affirms that God can effect such a change, although the word "move" is less apt than "transfer," since "movement" is normally used to refer to a change through a succession of points, and thus there seems to be a contradiction involved in saying that a body is moved, but not in time. Certainly God can so transfer a body, since succession due to the resistance of the movable thing or the medium is not inescapable. There can be no resistance to divine power. Here again Richard is whittling away at a possible argument for the necessity of transubstantiation, although he does not say so.

In another quodlibetal question, Richard explicitly asks whether the matter of the bread remains.[18] He replies that, according to Aristotle, when we say *hoc coelum* the word *hoc* signifies matter and form. When we say *hoc est corpus meum*, the reality designated by the word *hoc* comes from bread through transubstantiation. Thus the composite of matter and form is transubstantiated, and whoever says that the matter of the bread remains actually contradicts the truth of transubstantiation, which we learn from the Gospel. Furthermore, the common opinion of the masters, *sancti* and Roman church agrees that the accidents are without a subject in the eucharist. In short, we know that the matter does not remain because tradition teaches us to believe in transubstantiation. At no time does Richard try to argue that transubstantiation is, in turn, necessary for eucharistic presence.

In still another quodlibetal question, Richard asks whether God could transmute the dimensions of bread into the dimensions of Christ's body, and answers "without prejudice" that he could do so.[19] Two substances are no less distinguished from one another than two sets of dimensions. If God can effect such a transmutation in the former case—and the eucharist shows that he can—then he can do so in the latter case. To the objection that one body would then be locally present in several places at once, Richard suggests that two solutions are possible. On the one hand, one could answer that such need not be the case, for God could make Christ's body be related to the dimensions of bread, thus preventing it from being present locally. On the other hand, "one could answer, as others do, that what you consider contradiction is not such, for God can make a single body be locally present in various places."[20] Here again the discussion is,

---

[17] *Quodl.* II, a. 1, q. 2.
[18] *Quodl.* II, a. 1, q. 12.
[19] *Quodl.* II, q. 3.
[20] Ibid.: Alio modo potest dici secundum alios, quod illud quod tu habes pro inconvenienti non est inconveniens. Potest enim Deus facere unum corpus in diversis locis simul localiter secundum quod declaratum fuit in alio quodlibeto, et etiam confirmatum.

of course, entirely theoretical. Richard agrees that the dimensions of bread remain, and the dimensions of Christ's body are present through concomitance, as are his blood and soul.[21] Nevertheless, the discussion serves to underscore once again Richard's refusal to see any rational necessity beneath the present order of things.

We will now turn to another Franciscan scholar of some interest for our study, Vitalis de Furno. Vitalis' chronology is open to question, but he seems to have studied in Paris in the late 1280s or early 1290s under the Franciscan master Jacobus de Carceto. The fourth book of Vitalis' *Sentence* commentary has survived in a single *reportatio* which dates from 1295–96, when he was teaching at Montpellier; yet a note in the *reportatio* says that these Montpellier lectures were actually put together in Paris when he was studying under Jacobus de Carceto.[22] Valens Heynck takes the passage, "Iste quartus sententiarum fuit recollectus Parisius per magistrum fratrem Vitalis de Furno, . . . sub magistro fratre Jacobo de Carceto," to mean that Vitalis' views were based upon Jacobus.[23] If so, then Vitalis derived his views from a scholar whose student days would go back to the time when Richard of Middleton was a regent master.

The other source for Vitalis' eucharistic thought is his second *quodlibet*. Here the dating is complicated to some extent by a degree of uncertainty as to when he became a master. Although some scholars have assumed that he earned that status before he became lector at Montpellier in 1295, Heynck argues that it followed his teaching at Montpellier and Toulouse as well. Thus his quodlibetal questions must date from after 1297.[24]

In the second *quodlibet*, Vitalis asks whether the body of Christ can be in more than one *locus* at the same time.[25] He replies that "wise men differ with wise men on this issue." According to some, Christ's body can be in several places only sacramentally, by virtue of the fact that several things are converted into it. Others, say, however, that the conversion of the bread into Christ's body is not the cause of its being in several places. In the first place, the soul and dimensions of Christ's body are wherever the body is, and yet nothing is converted into either the soul or the dimensions. Second, the bread does not effect any new presence in Christ's body before the conversion, and certainly does not do so after the conversion, since it no longer remains. Third, the bread is converted into Christ's body, not the reverse, and hence it would seem to follow that the bread is where Christ's body was, not the reverse. Thus these scholars say that divine omnipotence, not conversion, is the cause of Christ's presence in several places.

In support of their position they cite Hugh of St. Victor's assertion that "he who made the body also made the place and put the body in the

---

[21] See *Quodl.* II, q. 11.

[22] See Valens Heynck, "Zur Busslehre des Vitalis de Furno," 163–66.

[23] See Ibid., p. 165 and Heynck's article "Vitalis von Furno," 819f.

[24] Heynck, "Zur Busslehre des Vitalis de Furno," 163. This is not far from the dating of Glorieux, *La Literature Quodlibetique*, II, 280, who dates the second *quodlibet* 1295–96.

[25] *Quodlibeta tria*, Rome, 1947, *Quodl.* II, q. 3, pp. 62–66.

place, and he who determined that one body should be in one place did as he wished, and if he had wished, he could have done otherwise, and he does otherwise when he wishes."[26]

Vitalis reports that these scholars go even further, arguing that God could change the dimensions of the bread into those of Christ's body, in which case Christ would be *localiter* in more than one *locus*. If it should be asked how such could be possible, they would answer that, as in the case of the virgin birth, it would be according to *rationes* which God has kept to himself and not communicated to his creatures.

If it should be argued against this position that only through either creation or some type of change (*mutatio*) can a body be where it previously was not, these scholars would answer that there is change of place, but not, as Aristotle would have it, involving the abandonment of the old place and the acquiring of a new one. The Aristotelian notion applies to natural change of place, but not to supernatural, where there can be acquisition of a new place without abandoning the old one. God, they say, can allow a body to be in two places at the same time just as he can allow two bodies to be in the same place simultaneously.

To the objection that a body could then be ubiquitous, which is proper only to God, Vitalis seems to reply that, according to these scholars, such is possible by divine power, yet the creature would not be everywhere in the same sense that God is everywhere.[27] To the objection that a thing in two places would be both equal to and twice the size of its place, scholars reply that the case is no different than when a body is successively in two places. To the objection that the view would involve contradictions, for a body finding itself in an oven in Paris—one wonders whether Vitalis received the desired smile from his students with the words *Parisius in furno*—and in the Tiber in Rome would be simultaneously hot and cold, these scholars answer that some properties affect the body absolutely without regard to place, others only in respect to place. Heat belongs in the first category and thus must be the same everywhere. Parisian fire and Roman water will both have their effect, but the result will be a single body temperature applying to the body in Paris and in Rome. The second category includes things like being touched, seen, etc., which can happen to a body in one place without occurring in another. Thus there is nothing contradictory about a body being moved in one place but not in another, which actually happens even in the case of eucharistic presence. To the objection that a body would thus be spatially distant from itself, for "things in place are spatially distant as the places are distant," they say that the words just quoted are true only of those things which are in a single place.

Vitalis drops the matter at this point, without explicitly declaring himself

---

[26] *De sacramentis*, lib. II, pars 8, cap. 11, *PL* 176, p. 469.

[27] *Quodl.* II, q. 3, p. 65. The manuscript actually says, "Dicunt quod sic virtute divina nec esse ubique quocumque modo est Dei proprietas, sed ubique totus intra, totus extra per se et propria virtute, et sic de aliis modis excessivis qui excedunt creaturam."

for either position. Nevertheless, it is hard to ignore the fact that the second one has received most of his attention.

Vitalis covers some of the same ground in his *Sentence* commentary, in the process of responding to the question of whether the body of Christ is actually contained under the species.[28] Nothing, he says, hinders such presence, for any such an impediment would have to be on the part of the body, the distance, or an intermediate cause. He then proceeds to dispose of all three, but it is only the second that should interest us. Distance is no impediment, he says, "for—as will appear in the reply to opposing arguments—God can make not only his own body but any other body be in several places at the same time without any contradiction being involved."[29]

The discussion thus promised by Vitalis appears in his response to the objection that nothing can begin to be present where it once was not unless there is some change, which cannot be affirmed of Christ's body. Vitalis notes that, according to some, the objection is largely true, but one important addition must be made. Nothing can be, without change, where it previously was not, unless something else is changed into it. In this case, a thing will begin to be where it was not, yet without any change except beginning to be in a new place.

This reply, Vitalis says, does not seem to be valid, for it is clear that the bread and wine are not converted into the soul of Christ, except through concomitance, and yet it, too, begins to be present wherever the conversion occurs.[30] Thus others say that the objection is true of created being which is not united to divine nature as the body and soul of Christ are, just as one can say "this is God" of no created being except that human nature assumed by the divinity.

This, too, Vitalis says, seems invalid, for if the body of Christ can be present in the eucharist because it is united with divinity, then for the same reason it can be said to be everywhere. Thus others say that the body of Christ, remaining in heaven, can begin to be present here because, in this place, the bread is converted into it, and it could not be present without change if such were not the case. These people say that it is impossible for the same body to be present in several places at once without contradictions ensuing. For example, if the same body were in Paris and Rome, it could be hot in one place and cold in the other, moved in one place and quiescent in the other.

Here again, Vitalis says, the reasoning is invalid, for there is no con-

---

[28] Ms. Vat. lat. 1095, ff. 12vb–13vb.

[29] Ibid., f. 13rb: Sicut enim patebit in solutione argumentorum deus non solum suum corpus sed etiam quodcumque aliud absque ulla contradictione vel repugnantia potest facere simul et semel esse in diversis locis.

[30] Ibid., f. 13va. A series of plurals in the second part of the sentence suggest that Vitalis mentions not only the soul but something else which is present by concomitance (perhaps the dimensions, as in the quodlibetal question), yet the latter has been eliminated through a scribal error.

tradiction involved in the notion of God making a body be present in
more than one place at a time without conversion. Although, according
to the normal course of nature, a body can occupy only one place at a
time, it remains true that God, the author of nature, can make his own
body or any other one be in several places at once, as Hugh of St. Victor
says. Vitalis disposes of the objection regarding contradictory accidents
by making the same sort of distinction seen in his quodlibetal question,
this time referring to intrinsic and extrinsic accidents. Intrinsic accidents
like heat cannot vary according to place, but extrinsic ones, which involve
a relationship with something outside the body, can do so.

Thus Vitalis clearly denies the necessity of transubstantiation for eucharistic presence; yet he does not deny the fact of transubstantiation, nor
does he fail to make use of substantial conversion as an explanatory tool.
Thus, in response to the objection that a body is necessarily three-di-
mensional and thus *situabile*, which cannot be the case with eucharistic
presence, he argues that the body is present *per modum solum substantiae*,
in such a way that quantity is truly present, but not *per modum quantitatis*.
In the following questions, he explains that Christ in the eucharist cannot
be seen by an angel or the virgin Mary, nor do the accidents of bread and
wine touch his body, for Christ is not present quantitatively or in the
manner of quantity, even though his whole substance and quantity is
present.[31] In the eucharist, Christ is present in the manner of substance,
which lacks all dimensions and does not have part outside of part. Instead,
the whole is in each part. "Thus those who picture the body of Christ
existing in the sacrament as dimensioned, having part outside of part, so
that the head can be seen and distinguished from the feet, etc., picture it
in an absurd and bestial manner and are thus deceived."[32] Vitalis goes on
to say that Christ's body in the eucharist "is freed (*absolutum*) from all
dimension and manner of quantity," a view intriguingly close to the one
combatted by Olivi. In a later question, however, Vitalis argues that it is
heretical to say the substance is present without its quantity, then refutes
an anonymous group of scholars who claim that quantity is present *per
se* and through conversion rather than through concomitance.[33] In his final
question on the eucharist, he extensively examines and refutes a view
according to which the substance of bread remains, entering into the form
of Christ's body and being actuated under it in such a way that it becomes
essentially one with it.[34] It must be held as certain, Vitalis concludes, "that
the substance of bread is neither annihilated nor remains, but changes
into the body of Christ."

[31] Ibid., ff. 13vb–14rb.
[32] Ibid.: Et ideo illi qui imaginantur quod corpus Christi ut in sacramento existens sit
dimensionatum et habeat partem extra partem ita quod possit vidi et distingui caput a pedibus
et sic de aliis phantastice imaginantur et bestialiter, et ideo decipiuntur.
[33] Ibid., ff. 16ra–rb.
[34] Ibid., 17vb–19ra, published as an appendix in Vitalis de Furno, *Quodlibeta tria*, pp.
211–16.

One final Franciscan theologian must be considered, and with him we are near the end of the century. Various suggestions have been offered regarding the date of William of Ware's *Sentence* commentary, but scholars tend to agree that there were at least three redactions, the earliest of which dates from sometime in the 1290s.[35] This earliest redaction was undoubtedly produced at Oxford, where his career may have overlapped with that of the young Duns Scotus. At any rate, according to fourteenth-century tradition, Ware was Scotus's teacher.[36]

In his *Sentence* commentary, William asks whether a creature can be transubstantiated into divinity.[37] His *videtur* section offering arguments for the positive answer is followed by a brief contra and a series of arguments by an anonymous *quidam* that such is impossible. William then observes, "I do not understand the truth of this matter, since I do not perfectly understand what is meant by the word 'transubstantiation'."[38] If, he says, nothing more is required for transubstantiation than that a thing be annihilated, it is hard to see why it cannot be said that something can be transubstantiated into divinity. "Nevertheless," Ware cautions, "I do not assert this view, but rather hold the opinion that a creature cannot be transubstantiated into divinity." Despite this fact, the arguments offered by the *quidam* do not hold, and Ware turns to refute them. Then he refutes the arguments of the *videtur* section.

Ware next asks whether a corporeal creature can be transubstantiated into a spiritual one.[39] Here he refutes arguments for the negative position and affirms that such is possible.

Ware now asks whether God can convert the substance of bread into that of Christ's body.[40] After a rather uneventful discussion of the problem in which he cites and refutes an argument from Giles of Rome's *Theoremata de corpore Christi*, he notes that, according to some, God cannot convert quantity into quantity, since the same body cannot be locally present in several places at once.

---

[35] See, among others, A. G. Little, "Franciscan School at Oxford," 866–68; Ephrem Longpré, "Maîtres Franciscaines de Paris, Guillaume de Ware," 71–82; Joseph Lechner, "Die mehrfachen Fassungen des Sentenzenkommentars des Wilhelm von Ware, O.F.M.," 14–31; Gedeon Gál, "Gulielmi de Ware, O.F.M., doctrina philosophica per summa capita proposita," 155–80, 265–92; P. Glorieux, "D'Alexandre de Hales à Pierre Auriol," 257–81; Aquilinus Emmen, "Wilhelm von Ware," 1154–56; Alfred Brotherton Emden, *Biographical Register of the University of Oxford to 1500,* 1986. For a list of the questions included in the Sentence commentary see Augustinus Daniels, "Zu den Beziehungen zwischen Wilhelm von Ware und Johannes Duns Scotus," 221–38.

[36] For the connection between the two men, see the articles by Gedeon Gál and Augustinus Daniels cited in the preceding footnote.

[37] Vat. lat. 4300, ff. 10ra–11ra. Although only this manuscript of Ware's commentary will be cited, it was compared with MSS. Padova Antoniana 115, Padova Antoniana 116, and Oxford Merton 103.

[38] Ibid., f. 10va: Quicquid sit de veritate questionis nescio, quia non intelligo perfecte quid impartetur per transubstantiationis nomen.

[39] Ibid., ff. 11ra–12ra.

[40] Ibid., ff. 12ra–vb.

William then summarizes Giles's argument against such a possibility. Nevertheless, he says, "I do not want to hold this position on the basis of such arguments," for if God should convert one quantity existing in the same place as Christ's body, it would not follow that his body would be in several places. Again, despite the fact that the quantity of bread was converted into that of Christ's body, his body could still be in the air and be related to the various parts of the air in a nonquantitative or nondimensive manner, as is now the case with sacramental presence. On the other hand, one can argue that there is no contradiction involved in a body being locally in several places.[41]

Ware now turns to the question of whether the body of Christ is actually under the sacrament,[42] and in doing so he finally addresses the main topic of this study. The truth of this matter is, of course, affirmed by the Christian faith, but he acknowledges that there is some difference as to how Christ's presence is to be described. Some say that Christ is present through the conversion of the bread into Christ's body. These people argue that the body of Christ must be present either through its own dimensions or through those of something else. It cannot be present through the former for a number of reasons. In the first place, the body would occupy more space than the host does. Second, in order to be present in a new place, it would have to travel through the intervening space. Just as it is impossible to travel from the past to the future except by going through the present, so it is impossible to travel from one point to another in space without passing through the intervening points. Again, being present under its own dimensions would mean being present in more than one place circumscriptively, which would imply a contradiction, since it is of the *ratio* of circumscriptive presence that no part of the substance be outside the *locus* where it is present. It follows, then, that Christ is in the sacrament through the dimensions of something else; yet such cannot be true unless it is present through conversion.[43]

Against this position, Ware remarks, it can be argued that, if it is implied in the *ratio* of circumscriptive presence that no part of what is circumscribed in one place can be contained outside that place, then it is a contradiction to say that Christ is circumscriptively in heaven and sacramentally on the altar. Sacramental presence implies that he is present according to substance and according to the same quantity, although not in a quantitative manner. Thus one would seem to be saying that Christ is and is not entirely within his *locus* in heaven.

---

[41] Ibid., f. 12 vb. The final thought, which seems to offer an alternative to the response Ware has just suggested, actually begins with the words *vel dicendum*. Thus my own paraphrase, "On the other hand, one can argue that," preserves the sense of an alternative explanation but does not do full justice to the Latin. A refutation of Aegidius Romanus, *Theoremata*, theorema 2, follows, but we need not pause here to examine it.

[42] Ibid., ff. 12vb–14rb.

[43] Ibid., f. 13ra–rb. I have rearranged the argument slightly. The assertion regarding circumscriptive presence is actually introduced last and seems intended to explain why things can be present through alien dimensions only by conversion.

Ware cites the objection that when water is converted into wine, the water is more likely to be said to be in the place of the wine than the reverse. Thus, if the bread is converted into the body of Christ, it seems that it ought to be said that the bread is in heaven through this conversion rather than the reverse. It would follow, then, that the body cannot be on the altar through conversion.

Ware notes that the example is a bad one, for the reason why the water is said to be in the place of the wine is that, in order to be converted into wine, it is placed in the *locus* where the wine is. Thus the conversion is not the cause of the water being in that particular *locus*. In the case of eucharistic conversion, the bread is not first placed in heaven.

Nevertheless, the subject of conversion as a causal factor in eucharistic presence remains an important one, and Ware continues to probe it. He argues at one point that whatever God can do as an efficient cause working through a creature, he can do *per se*, without the creature. Thus, if He can make the body of Christ be present on the altar through conversion, He can do the same thing without conversion, just as He can produce heat directly without using fire.[44]

Shortly thereafter, Ware gives the same subject a slightly different treatment. If conversion is to be considered the cause of Christ's presence on the altar, it must be either the material, formal, efficient or final cause. It cannot be the material cause, nor can it be the efficient cause, since only divine power is the efficient cause. Nor can it be the final cause, since conversion is said to take place for the sake of presence rather than the reverse. Thus, if it is a cause, it must be a formal cause; yet this, too, is impossible. If present conversion were taken as the formal cause, the body of Christ would be present only so long as the act of conversion lasted. If past conversion were the formal cause, the body of Christ would not cease to be present when the species were corrupted.[45]

Ware is now ready to sum up his thoughts on the causal role of conversion. Conversion is not the cause of Christ's simple existence on the altar, "although it is now in fact the cause of its existing in a certain way, that is, in a manner neither dimensional nor quantitative." Even in this limited sphere, however, it is not a necessary cause. God could make the body be present on the altar according to its quantity, but in a nonquantitative manner, without any conversion whatsoever. As to the opposing arguments, in response to the assertion that the body of Christ must be present in the eucharist through its own dimensions or through those of something else, William replies that the body, a substance, does not exist in a place through quantity, for quantity does not give existence in a place *simpliciter*, but only a manner of existing. The body of Christ is present *effective* through divine power and *formaliter* through its substance. That it is present in a certain manner, i.e. unextended, comes about through

---

[44] Ibid., f. 13ra.
[45] Ibid., f. 13va.

conversion of the substance of bread into the substance of Christ's body, for the quantity of the body is there, not *ex vi conversionis*, but only concomitantly. Quantity thus has the mode of being proper to substance, which exists entirely in each part of quantity. On the other hand, it can be argued that (another *vel dicendum* clause) the body of Christ is not present through the quantity of something else (*per quantitatem alienam*), but rather is present under the quantity of something else (*sub quantitate aliena*), which is a different matter.

As for the analogy between time and space assumed by the opposing position, Ware argues that they are not similar at all. One cannot go from past to future without passing through the present, but God can move a thing from one *locus* to another without making it pass through any intervening space. It could also be argued (another *vel dicendum* clause) that time and place differ inasmuch as it is the same time which is past, present and future. The same time is *in potentia* in the future, *in actu* in the present, then *in potentia* once again in the past. Thus it is impossible for it to be future and then past without being present.

As to the argument concerning circumscriptive presence, Ware again observes that it can be turned against his opponents' own position, ruling out the possibility of Christ being circumscriptively present in heaven and sacramentally present in the eucharist. Thus it must be said that there is a positive circumscription, according to which part of the located thing is conjoined with part of the *locus*, and there is a negative circumscription, according to which what is here cannot be elsewhere. That which is limited in power cannot surmount this negative circumscription, but divine power can do so.

As to the argument that Christ must be present through change in something else and therefore through conversion of the bread into itself, since it cannot be present through change in itself (i.e. through change of place), Ware answers that the body of Christ is, in fact, present through change in itself because it is where it formally was not. Alternatively, one can say (*vel dicendum*) that, if "change in itself" and "change in something else" are both taken to refer to the conversion, the body of Christ is present neither through change of place nor through conversion.

Ware examines the question of whether the same bread can return without any change in the body of Christ,[46] then turns to an examination of whether Christ is circumscriptively present.[47] In dealing with the latter, he affirms that the substance of Christ's body is present *ex vi sacramenti*, as is seen from the words of consecration, which more immediately refer to the corporeal substance than to the intellectual soul or quantity. It follows that, as soon as the body of Christ is present, the divinity which sustains it is also there; for, although the divinity is everywhere, it is not everywhere as sustaining such a nature. Again, since Christ's body is a

---

[46] Ibid., ff. 14rb–vb.
[47] Ibid., ff. 14vb–15vb.

living substance, the intellectual soul is the act of the organized body, and there can be no organization without quantity, it follows that the soul and the quantity are also present.

Ware later notes that the body of Christ is not present *mediante quantitate,* but that the dimensions are present *mediante substantia.* Thus the dimensions of the bread can be present with those of the body, the normal cause of such resistance being removed. Moreover, since the whole body of Christ is present where any single part is, it is not present in a dimensive manner, with part outside of part insofar as it exists in a place and is configured or commensurated with that place. In short, it is not circum-scriptively present.

Ware now asks whether the body of Christ is entirely in the whole host and in each part.[48] He cites and rejects the view according to which such is true only after the host is broken. In reply to the argument that the surface of the host is in infinite parts and thus, if Christ were in every part, an actual infinity would follow, Ware acknowledges that mathematical quantity can be divided into infinite parts, but insists that the remaining quantity is not mathematical quantity. Although, like mathematical quan-tity, it is separate from matter, it is not separate from *sensibilitas,* or the ability to be sensed, as is mathematical quantity. Quantity in the eucharist is infinite *in potentia,* not *in actu,* so there is no contradiction involved.

To the objection that such an arrangement would put Christ's hand where his eye is, William responds that order of the parts in the whole is different from order of the parts in place. He offers the example of a man turned upside down, with his feet higher in relation to place yet always lower in relation to the whole. Again, he invokes rays of the sun, moon and stars, which are indistinct in relation to the medium in which they exist together yet are distinct and unconfused in relation to their origin.

Later in his commentary, Ware asks whether the bread transubstantiated into the body of Christ is annihilated.[49] In the *videtur* section, he presents a series of arguments that it is not. Annihilation is a different sort of change than transubstantiation, and if a process is one it cannot be the other. Again, if a thing is transformed into another form it is not annihilated, nor does it begin not to be; and the same thing would apply to what is transubstantiated. Again, that which is transmuted into something nobler is not annihilated.

Against these arguments, Ware offers several affirming annihilation. Whatever exists is somewhere and thus remains, but that of which nothing remains in existence is annihilated. Again, if through change matter as well as form ceases to be, the substance is annihilated. Again, that which is not annihilated remains in some way, either potentially or actually. Here the bread does not actually remain, nor can it remain potentially, since

---

[48] Ibid., ff. 15vb–16rb.
[49] Ibid., ff. 18ra–19va.

the body of Christ, being incorruptible, cannot be *in potentia* to a cor-
ruptible form.

As Ware moves on to the *responsio* section of the question, the debate
continues. Those who deny annihilation, he says, offer several arguments
for their position. For example, they say that anything which begins to
be present in some place becomes such through motion on its own part
or through change in something else. Thus the body of Christ must come
to be present in the eucharist either by local motion, which cannot be the
case, or by conversion of something else into itself. If the bread were
annihilated, nothing would be changed into the body of Christ. Thus it
is contradictory to say that the body of Christ is present and that the bread
is annihilated.

Again, creation and annihilation are opposite changes. The *terminus a
quo* of creation is negative and the *terminus ad quem* is positive. Precisely
the opposite is true for annihilation. The *terminus ad quem* of transubstantiation is positive rather than negative, and thus the bread is not
annihilated.

Other arguments follow, but Ware caps them with still another argument
for annihilation which suggests that transubstantiation and annihilation
are compatible. Thus, he says, there is another opinion which holds that
the bread is annihilated in such a way that conversion immediately falls
on a negative *terminus* and not on a positive one. Although a positive
term follows the negative one, that fact does not erase the *ratio* of annihilation from a conversion the earliest and most immediate term of
which is pure nothingness. For example, suppose God annihilated air and
yet always, after doing so, put fire where the air had been. Likewise, in
the present case, although through divine power there always follows a
presence (*positio*) of Christ's body in the place where the bread formerly
was, the bread is annihilated, since nothing of it remains and there is no
addition to the body of Christ, which remains as it was before the conversion.

Ware sees the implications of the position and traces them out. If transubstantiation is nothing more than annihilation of something and a presence (*positio*) of something else, then it is possible for the bread to be
transubstantiated into divinity, for God can certainly annihilate the bread
and then effect the presence (*positio*) of divinity in the same place.

As to the argument against annihilation based on a limitation of alternatives to local motion and conversion, Ware replies that God can make
Christ be present without either conversion or local motion, in fact without
any change (*mutatio*) whatsoever except regarding place. As to the next
argument, Ware states that there are two changes (*mutationes*) involved
in transubstantiation. One is an alteration (*versio*) the immediate term of
which is nothing. The other change is one of simple position, the immediate
term of which is positive.

Ware continues to work his way carefully through the objections to
annihilation, refuting them one by one. Finally he comes to the point

where he must offer some sort of conclusion. "Nevertheless," he says, "because of the authority of the *sancti*, who say expressly that the bread is not annihilated, even though I may not understand this perfectly, I wish to hold my understanding captive and be one with the *sancti* in saying that it is not annihilated."[50] He quotes Hugh of St. Victor and John Damascene, then searches for an example. When possible form is reduced to act, the possible form remains in the actual form, although it does not remain as possible. If such is the case, then *a fortiori* God can make one actual form remain in another. Thus, through transubstantiation, the bread remains in some way in the body of Christ, "although I confess that I cannot understand how it does so."

Ware now turns to the final task of refuting the arguments for annihilation. To the first offered in the earlier part of the question he replies that something is annihilated if it does not remain anywhere either in itself or in something else. The bread does in fact remain insofar as it is in the body of Christ. In response to the third argument he again returns to this point, arguing that the bread must remain in the body of Christ in some way. In a sense, one could say that it remains potentially, for, just as God converts the bread into Christ's body, he could reverse the process and convert the body into bread. On the other hand, one could say that *in potentia* and *in actu* are the two natural ways of remaining, but the bread does not remain in a natural way. Again, one could say that the bread remains in the body of Christ in a certain way on account of which the same bread can return without a reverse transubstantiation taking place at the time the species are corrupted.

---

[50] The quotation given here is a composite drawn from several manuscripts: "Verumptamen propter autoritates sanctorum que dicunt expresse quod panis non annihilatur, et si non intelligam hoc perfecte, nihilominus tamen captivando intellectum meum dico una cum sanctis volo dicere quod non adnihilatur." Vat. lat. 4300, f. 19ra actually omits "captivando intellectum meum dico," saying "nihilominus una cum sanctis volo dicere."

VII. THE FRANCISCAN CRITIQUE:
JOHN DUNS SCOTUS

The chronology of John Duns Scotus's career is the subject of some uncertainty. Whereas Callebaut,[1] Little,[2] Balić[3] and others have posited a Paris education during the 1290s, Brampton[4] argues that Scotus's theological education began at Oxford in 1288 and continued there until June, 1301. In any case, it is generally recognized that Scotus lectured on the *Sentences* at Oxford and was already working on the *Opus Oxoniense* by 1300, although there is notable difference of opinion as to whether he lectured on all four books of the *Sentences* as a bachelor at Oxford and precisely when he lectured on them.[5] Moreover, it is widely agreed that he began reading the *Sentences* at Paris in the fall of 1302 and that these lectures were the source of the commentary now referred to as the *Reportata Parisiensia*, although there is controversy as to the order in which he proceeded.[6] Scotus was recommended by the minister general as a candidate for the magisterium in November, 1304,[7] and probably received that status the following year, serving as regent master in 1306 and 1307.[8]

It was as a regent master that Scotus produced his quodlibetal questions, which probably date from Advent, 1306, or Lent, 1307.[9] He probably also continued work on his *Opus Oxoniense* during this period. In 1307 he was transferred to Cologne, where he died in 1308.[10]

If this basic outline can be trusted, then three works relevant to the eucharist can be traced to the last five or six years of Scotus's life: The *Opus Oxoniense, Reportata Parisiensia*, and quodlibetal questions. This fact will complicate our examination much less than one might at first imagine, since these works, while they do not entirely agree, do not differ sharply enough to merit separate examination, except on one issue which will be dealt with in its place. We shall concentrate on the *Opus Oxoniense* (which

---

[1] A. Callebaut, "Le bx. Jean Duns Scot étudiant à Paris," 3–12.
[2] A. G. Little, "Chronological Notes on the Life of Duns Scotus," 571.
[3] Charles Balić, "The Life and Works of John Duns Scotus," 10f.
[4] C. K. Brampton, "Duns Scotus at Oxford, 1288–1301," 5–20.
[5] See Balić, "Life and Works," pp. 11f; Brampton, "Duns Scotus," 18f.
[6] See Balić, "Life and Works," p. 12; Brampton, "Duns Scotus," 12–15.
[7] See A. Callebaut, "La maîtrise du Bx. Jeans Duns Scot en 1305," 209.
[8] See Little "Chronological Notes," 581.
[9] See the introduction to John Duns Scotus, *God and Creatures*, ed. Felix Alluntis and Allen Wolter, Princeton, Princeton University Press, 1975, xxvii.
[10] See W. Lampen, "B. Ioannes Duns Scotus, Lector coloniensis," 297–300.

Charles Balić describes as reflecting "Scotus' final and definitive doctrine"),[11] citing other works when necessary.

Scotus asks in his *Opus Oxoniense* "whether it is possible for the body of Christ to be really contained under the species of bread and wine."[12] Having acknowledged that such is an article of faith, he turns to investigate "how that which is believed is possible." This question is divided in turn into two more specific questions. First, how can the body of Christ begin to be present on the altar without change of place (*mutatio localis*)? Second, how can the body be a *quantum*, a quantified thing, without being present in a quantitative manner?

"As to the first question," Scotus says, "it is commonly stated that such occurs through change of something else into the body of Christ, that is, because of the conversion of bread into Christ's body." Thus it is not necessary for the body to be changed.[13] Against this view he argues that the *per se terminus ad quem* of transubstantiation is substance, and nothing posterior to the *per se terminus ad quem* can be a result of transubstantiation. Thus, since the presence of the substance is posterior to the substance itself, it cannot come about through transubstantiation. The same conclusion can be reached if the notion of otherness (*alienitas*) is substituted for that of posteriority. Nothing which is, in itself, other than the *per se terminus* of a change can be produced by that change. Presence is other than substance, and therefore substantial change does not necessarily entail presence.

Second, God could make his body be present along with the bread, for a change in what is posterior does not demand one in what is prior. This presence would be of the same sort as that now enjoyed by Christ's body. Therefore this presence comes about through something other than substantial change. If one should say that God could make Christ be present along with the bread, yet now in fact makes him be present through eucharistic conversion, it can be replied that God could convert the bread into the body of Christ already present along with the bread, in which case Christ would not be present through the conversion.

Third, what is converted into a preexistent thing is more apt to acquire the conditions of that thing than the reverse. If food is converted into

---

[11] Balić, "Life and Works," 21.

[12] *Opus Oxoniense*, IV, d. 10, q. 1, in *Opera*, Lyons, Laurentius Durand, 1639, VIII, pp. 487–508. The same question is asked in the *Reportata Parisiensia*, IV, d. 10, q. 1, in *Opera*, XI. 2, pp. 632–36. This is perhaps a good moment to note that the Paris, J. Granion, 1517–18 edition of the Scotus *Reportata super primum* (. . . *quartum*) *sententiarum* offers a text notably different from the one cited here. The problem of this edition has been discussed by Balić and need not be explored here except to note that, on the issues important for this study, the Paris, 1518 edition is essentially at one with the *Reportata Parisiensia* as cited from the Lyons, 1639 *Opera*, although a more detailed comparison reveals some striking differences.

[13] *Op. Oxon.*, p. 498: De primo dicitur communiter, quod hoc est propter mutationem alterius in ipsum, puta propter conversionem panis in corpus Christi; et ideo non oportet ipsum corpus in se mutari: sufficit enim, quod aliud mutetur in ipsum ad hoc, quod incipiat corpus ibi praesentialiter esse.

flesh, the food acquires the conditions of the flesh, including its location. Thus one would expect that, through conversion of bread into the preexistent body of Christ, the converted bread would acquire presence in heaven rather than Christ acquiring presence on the altar.

Fourth, God could convert the bread into the body of Christ as it is present in heaven, for there is no more contradiction involved here than in what is presently posited. In that case, the body of Christ would not be present under the species of bread through conversion. Therefore, it is not so at present.

Fifth, if quantified bread were converted into the quantified body of Christ in such a way that quantity were converted into quantity and substance into substance, the quantified body of Christ would not have the same circumscriptive location possessed by the bread, since it is bigger than the bread. As quantified substances are related to place circumscriptively, so substances in themselves are related to place definitively. Thus the substance of Christ's body is not in place definitively through substantial conversion.[14]

Thus, Scotus says, "one need not flee to conversion" in order to explain eucharistic presence. He himself chooses to attack the problem in a strikingly different way. He begins with an analysis of what sorts of change are involved in the action of becoming present. When a body is moved from one place to another, expelling another body in the process, four changes (*mutationes*) and eight terms (*termini*) are involved. First, there is a change in the expelling body from presence in a certain place to loss of that presence; second, there is change in the same body from lack of presence in the new place to acquisition of such presence; third, there is a change in the expelled body from presence in the old place to lack of such. Finally, there is change in the expelled body from lack of presence in a new place to acquisition of such presence. When a body moves from place to place without expelling another body, two changes and four terms are involved. When it gains a new place without leaving the old one, one acquisitive change between two terms is sufficient. Here one reaches the absolute minimum of changes possible in the gaining of any new place.

Thus the body of Christ becomes present in the eucharist, not (as some have affirmed) without any change at all, but through a single acquisitive change. Scotus emphasizes that this change does not alter the form of Christ's body. It simply involves the acquisition of a new *respectus extrinsecus adveniens*.[15]

---

[14] *Op. Oxon.*, pp. 498f. All five arguments are found in the *Rep. Par.*, p. 633.

[15] *Op. Oxon.*, pp. 501f. After considering a series of awkward translations, I have decided that the term *respectus extrinsecus adveniens* might just as well stay in Latin. In essence, it refers to a relation of one thing to another, but a relation of such a sort that it is not directly determined by the natures of the things in question. In other words, the respectus can be added or subtracted without altering the nature of either thing. As we will see, Scotus' formulation of eucharistic presence is heavily dependent upon his essentially "realistic" notion of a *respectus extrinsecus adveniens*. His treatment of the problem in the *Rep. Par.*, p.

Scotus now turns to the second question, that of how a body can be a quantified thing without being present in a quantified manner. "It is said that the quantity of Christ's body is under the species of bread only concomitantly, for the first term of conversion is the substance of Christ's body, and whatever is there is present in the manner in which the conversion is terminated." Therefore the quantity will be present in the manner of substance, and thus in a nonquantitative manner.

Scotus counters that anything which is really present must be present with all the attributes which naturally and necessarily belong to it. Whether God creates a substance or nature generates it with concomitant quantity, the first term in each case is substance with concomitant quantity. In each case, quantity will have its own manner of existing.[16]

Another solution, he says, would argue that the body of Christ is present without extension of parts. Scotus does not linger over this view, but dismisses it with the observation that it is not *probabile*, since it denies to the body of Christ that *positio* and *figura* necessary to any animated body.[17]

Scotus's use of the word *positio* offers a preview of his own solution. If his answer to the first question proceeds from an analysis of change, his answer to the second proceeds from an analysis of position. He distinguishes position as a *differentia* of quantity (involving an order of parts in the whole) from position as a predicament (involving an order of parts to a place).[18] Position in the first sense is necessarily present in any quantified thing. Position in the second sense is not. A quantified thing may be deprived of the latter through God's omnipotence, by simple negation of any place. If, for example, God were to place a cat outside the universe, it would still have internal order of parts—its nose would still be in front of its tail and between its whiskers—but these parts would not be ordered to any place, since the cat would not be present in any place. The important thing for Scotus, however, is that such a negation of any place is not required in order for a thing to be without position in the second sense. The cat could be present to a given place in a way that there was not commensuration or coextension of the parts of the cat with the parts of the place, for such would be nothing more than the presence of one *respectus extrinsecus adveniens*, the coexistence of one thing with another, in the absence of another *respectus extrinsecus adveniens*, coextension of the parts of one with those of another.[19]

How, then, is this distinction to be applied to the case at hand? Scotus's

---

634, is similar. Here he speaks of a maximum of two changes and four terms, but his basic approach is the same and he uses the term *respectus extrinsecus adveniens*.

[16] *Op. Oxon.*, 503. *Rep. Par.*, 633f. is similar.

[17] *Op. Oxon.*, 503f; *Rep. Par.*, 635.

[18] The distinction is hardly foreign to earlier scholastics. In his *Commentaria in octo libros physicorum Aristotelis*, liber 4, lectio 7, in *Opera*, 2 Thomas distinguished between *situs* as a predicament (involving *ordo partium in loco*) and *situs* as a *differentia quantitatis* (involving *ordo partium in toto*).

[19] *Op. Oxon.*, 505f. See *Rep. Par.*, 635.

argument is somewhat obscured by the complexity of his terminology. Having distinguished between the two senses of *positio,* he comments that the second sense, *positio* as a predicament, is what is called the quantitative or dimensive mode of existence. Had he stopped at this point, the discussion might have retained at least the appearance of clarity. Unfortunately he chooses to make four more distinctions. First, there is the aforementioned distinction between coexistence and coextension (or commensuration). Next, there is a distinction between *ubi,* which is a *respectus extrinsecus* of the whole circumscribed thing to the whole circumscribing thing (e.g. of the whole cat to the whole *locus* in which the cat is present), and *positio,* which "adds (*superaddit*) a *respectus* of parts to parts." Third, there is a distinction between coexistence and *ubi.* Finally, there is a distinction between simple presence (*praesentia simplex*) and *ubi.*

How does one go about fitting all of these distinctions into a coherent pattern? The first sense of position can be dispensed with at once, since it is intrinsic to the substance and obviously has nothing to do with the other categories, which are described as *respectus extrinsecus advenientes.* The second sense of *positio, positio* as a predicament, can be identified with that position which is contrasted with *ubi.* Both of these can, in turn, be identified with coextension.

The other pieces of the puzzle are a bit harder to fit together, but it can be done. The difficulty lies partly in the fact that Scotus is trying to describe a phenomenon which cannot be classified within the context of the Aristotelian predicaments as Scotus himself understands them. The sort of presence he envisages for Christ in the eucharist is described by him as coexistence or simple presence. Such presence is not equivalent to the predicament *positio,* since there is no coextension of parts involved. Thus he is left with a single possibility, the predicament *ubi.* While he grants that eucharistic presence might be referred "more properly" to this predicament than to any other, he is unwilling to assign it there unconditionally, since he sees *ubi* as presence in a single place, while eucharistic presence involves presence in two or more places at once.[20] Thus he seems to be heading toward a threefold distinction according to which presence can be simple, definitive (i.e. limited to one place) or circumscriptive (i.e. with coextension of parts). Such is, in fact, precisely the solution offered by the Scotist Johannes de Bassolis,[21] but Scotus himself is less definite about the matter.[22]

---

[20] . . . praesentia corporis Christi speciei magis recedit a vera ratione ubi, quia nullo modo per istam praesentiam determinatur sic ad unum ubi, quod sibi repugnat aliud.

[21] *In librum sententiarum opus* (Paris, 1517), IV, d. 10, q. 1, fol. 38r, Johannes sees all three types as contained within the predicament *ubi.*

[22] He remarks that the divergence between eucharistic presence and the predicament *ubi* does not necessarily suggest the existence of more than ten predicaments, but may simply reflect our failure to define the ten as satisfactorily as we might. See also Scotus's *Quaestiones quodlibetales,* q. 11, where he limits the notion of *ubi* properly speaking to *praesens modo quantitativo* or as *coextensum loco,* but grants that the presence of the whole to *cuilibet parti illius loci*—as in the case of angelic presence—may improperly be called *ubi.*

In reality, Scotus's argument is sufficient for his own purposes. He has contrasted the intrinsic sense of quantity and position with the extrinsic one. In terms of the first, the body of Christ by virtue of its very nature is of a different shape and size than the eucharistic species; yet no particular form of *respectus extrinsecus adveniens* follows from this fact. That is, the fact implies no limitation to a single place and no particular type of commensuration or coextension of the parts of Christ's body with the parts of a *locus*. Thus the body of Christ has one part outside of another in itself, but it does not follow that it has one part outside of that part of the *locus* in which another part is located.

There is a great deal of truth in Reinhold Seeberg's observation that Scotus, while apparently complicating the problem, has actually simplified it.[23] His distinction between two senses of *positio* enables him to separate the problem of the shape and size of Christ's body from that of how it is present in a particular place, and the latter problem is neutralized, if not completely solved, by his classification of presence in terms of different types of *respectus extrinsecus adveniens*. Christ is present in the eucharist by a simple presence which implies neither limitation to a single place nor presence in a quantitative mode.

Useful as this notion of simple presence may be for Scotus, it is not a prerequisite for multiple presence. It follows from Scotus's understanding of a *respectus extrinsecus adveniens* that Christ could be present in several places at once in a quantitative manner. So, for that matter, could our aforementioned cat. There is nothing special about Christ in this regard. In a question on whether the same body can be locally present in several places at once,[24] Scotus begins by presenting the arguments of an anonymous *doctor* against the possibility. First, multiple local presence would imply the possibility of ubiquity, which is proper to God alone. Second, various contradictions would follow, such as the body being cold in one place and warm in another; hungry in one place and satiated in another; ill in one place and healthy in another; or dead in one place and alive in another. Again, just as a located thing is commensurated with the dimensions of the place as to size and continuity, it is commensurated with it according to unity and diversity. Thus a thing in two places would be both one and many.

Another anonymous doctor argues that the boundaries (*termini*) of the place and the located thing are the same, and therefore, if a located thing is outside the boundaries of its place, it is outside its own boundaries and therefore outside itself. Still another doctor argues that, just as a thing is in only one species through its own nature, so it is only in one place through its own dimensions, since quantity is related to place as nature is related to species. Another affirms that, if the same thing should be

---

[23] *Die Theologie des Johannes Duns Scotus,* 271.
[24] *Op. Oxon.,* 508ff.

present in several places it would come to be such by one or two changes (*mutationes*). It could not be by one, since that could lead to only one term. Nor could it be by two, since these would have to be of the same or different species. The former is impossible, for the same thing cannot be moved by two motions of the same species at the same time, as Aristotle says. The latter is also impossible, for the terms would then be contrary and the motions contradictory.

Having presented other people's arguments against the possibility of multiple local presence, Scotus adds a few of his own and then refutes them all. He first appeals to God's omnipotence. All that does not include an evident contradiction or from which an evident contradiction does not follow is possible for God. This appeal hardly settles anything by itself, of course, since it must still be demonstrated that the matter in question does not imply a contradiction. In attempting to demonstrate that such is the case, Scotus first argues by way of a comparison with the simultaneous presence of two bodies in one place. Such a phenomenon, no less contradictory than the one now being discussed, actually occurred after Christ's resurrection when Christ's body was given the *dos subtilitatis*.[25]

Scotus realizes that he is offering an objection already answered by the doctor whose arguments he quoted earlier. According to that doctor, the repugnance between two dimensions is removed by the gift of subtlety, but the impossibility of simultaneous local presence cannot be removed, for even a glorified body has determined *situs* which demands that it be in one place and not elsewhere. Scotus responds to this objection by asserting that the doctor's third argument against presence in several places would apply equally well to the presence of several things in one place. Since the place must be commensurated with the located thing as well as the reverse, the same contradictions would apply to the *locus* in the case of several things in one place as would apply to the *locatum* in the case of presence in several places.[26] Thus the former is just as impossible as the latter.

Scotus now presents a second argument: It is possible for God to convert the quantity of the bread into that of Christ's body. Since, according to the doctor in question, that into which something is converted begins to be present where that which was converted used to be, and since, according to him, a thing cannot be present according to its quantity without being locally present, it follows that such a conversion would result in the body being locally present. Such a conversion could be repeated on more than one altar.

Scotus acknowledges that the anonymous doctor has a reply to such an argument. If the substance of bread should remain in such a conversion,

---

[25] *Op. Oxon.*, 511. *Rep. Par.*, p. 637 mentions both post-resurrection phenomena and the virgin birth.

[26] *Op. Oxon.*, p. 511. *Rep. Par.*, p. 638 presents this argument even more clearly. Note that Scotus actually uses words like *inconveniens* and *impossibile*. He does not try to temper them with some adjective like "apparent."

it would follow either that it was informed by the dimensions of Christ's body, in which case the body of Christ would still be dimensively in only one place; or that the bread was not informed by these dimensions, in which case the body of Christ would be where the substance of the bread is only by reason of that substance and thus not in a dimensional manner or locally. If, on the other hand, the entire bread, substance and quantity, were converted into the entire body of Christ, nothing would remain by reason of which the body could be said to be present where the bread used to be.

Scotus pauses a moment to fortify his argument by inviting us to imagine that a quantified substance precisely equal to the body of Christ is being converted, then he plunges into the most important aspect of his counter-attack. If one accepts the proposition that the term of the conversion begins to be present where the converted thing used to be, it is fruitless to argue that, given a conversion of substance and quantity into substance and quantity, nothing will remain by reason of which the body will be present. Scotus observes that the question does not trouble him much, since he thinks the proposition is false in any case.

Scotus announces that he will argue the same point in a third way: "Wherever God can make a natural substance exist in an unnatural manner, he can make it exist in a natural manner." The former would involve two miracles, the second only one. Thus if God can make Christ exist sacramentally in the eucharist, he can make him exist there naturally, which is to say locally and dimensionally.

It is pointless to protest that Christ is present through conversion of something else into his body, for conversion is not the formal cause of his presence. If it were, Christ would not remain present after the act of conversion takes place. Nor is there any value in saying that the remaining species are the reason why Christ exists there, for these species are not formally in the body of Christ and cannot be the cause of Christ's formal existence in that place. Thus the body is formally present through something other than conversion or remaining species, "as Hugh says, who attributes all to divine power."

Fourth, Scotus argues, an angel can be definitively present in several places at once, since God could convert bread into an angel. Thus a body can be circumscriptively such, since "there is a similar *habitudo* in each and thus a similar determination to place, although each in a manner fitting to it.

"Of these four arguments," Scotus observes, "I would value the first and third." The second and fourth proceed from a proposition which he does not consider to be true, although they work well against those who do hold that proposition. Scotus insists that his view is consonant with Hugh of St. Victor's, since Hugh attributes multiple presence to divine omnipotence and not to conversion.[27]

---

[27] *Op. Oxon.*, 511–13. *Rep. Par.*, 637–39, offers the first three arguments.

Thus such multiple presence lies within the realm of divine omnipotence, for it involves nothing more than a multiplication of *respectus intrinsecus advenientes*.

Scotus is now ready to present his conclusion, and in doing so he finally translates the whole matter into his own understanding of presence. Presence in several places at once involves nothing more than the multiplication of *respectus extrinsecus advenientes*. Those who choose to follow their imaginations may find it difficult to imagine how such *respectus* can be multiplied, but those who follow reason will see that such is quite possible, for such *respectus* of place are posterior to the things being placed, and are clearly accidental and contingent to them. Certainly the multiplication of *respectus extrinsecus advenientes* is no less possible than that of *respectus intrinsecus advenientes*; yet the latter can indeed be multiplied, as is seen in the fact that two different relations of similarity can relate a single white thing to two other white things. Such an observation should give the modern reader pause, for it represents one of the moments when Scotus's theoretical edifice, his Gothic cathedral of the mind, can be viewed in very graphic terms. He is saying that, if our aforementioned cat can be the same color as several other cats, then *a fortiori* he can sit on several front porches at the same time.[28]

Scotus's reactions to some of his opponents' objections are worth noting, at least in passing. To the objection that multiple local presence would imply the possibility of ubiquity, Scotus replies that the same persons grant the possibility of Christ being everywhere sacramentally, since they would agree that God could convert everything in the world into his body. Sacramental ubiquity would seem to present no less a problem than local ubiquity. As to the assertion that only God is ubiquitous, God is such through his immensity, for nothing can be anywhere without God being present to it according to his power, presence, and essence. Nothing but God can be ubiquitous in this sense, but that does not prevent something else from being present everywhere through God's power.

As to the possible contradictions involved in multiple presence, Scotus notes that the example of cold and heat presents no more problem than if they were both applied to the object in the same place. In either case, they would contend against one another to produce a single temperature in the body. As to hunger and thirst, insofar as they are natural appetites they are absolute attributes which would not vary according to location. Thus, if the body ate well in one location, it would be satiated everywhere. On the other hand, if satiety is thought of as a fullness of the stomach, then one is dealing with a *respectus extrinsecus*, the presence of the food in the containing stomach, in which case nothing absolute is involved. The notion of absolute versus relative attributes is applied to each of the other cases mentioned in the objection.[29]

---

[28] *Op. Oxon.*, 513ff. See *Rep. Par.*, 639f.
[29] *Op. Oxon.*, 518f. See *Rep. Par.*, 640f., where the argument is slightly different.

To the objection regarding commensuration of a thing with its place, Scotus replies that plurality of the latter does not imply plurality of the former, for multiplication of what is posterior does not imply multiplication of what is prior, especially when one is dealing with *respectus extrinsicus advenientes*. To the argument regarding *termini,* he responds that the *termini* of one thing can be understood to be together (*simul*) with those of another either with precise and equal simultaneity (*simultate praecisa et adaequata*) or with simultaneity that is not such. If the latter, then it does not follow that what is outside the *termini* of one will be outside those of the other, for if a thing is together with something larger than itself it does not follow that what is together with one will be together with the other.

In reply to the argument that a thing is in only one place through its own dimensions just as it is in only one species through its own nature, Scotus notes that the nature of a thing is the formal reason for its being in a species, whereas dimension is not the immediate formal reason (*ratio formalis proxima*) why a thing is in a place, but merely the fundamental reason (*ratio fundamentalis*). The final objection regarding the number of *mutationes* required for multiple presence is answered with a long and involved counterthrust which, happily, can be ignored at present.

Scotus manages to return to the question of multiple local presence in the following question, where he asks whether Christ's body can be in heaven and in the eucharist simultaneously.[30] He answers that, according to one view, such can be the case only because it is sacramentally present in the eucharist through conversion, since simultaneous local presence would involve a contradiction. This view is false, however, since it is clear that neither conversion nor the eucharistic species are the formal cause of Christ's presence. Again, the presence of Christ's body along with the substance of bread is no more repugnant than its presence with the accidents of bread. Thus God could make Christ be present without conversion. Again, if God can make something be in several places in a manner not natural to it, certainly he can make it be present in those places in its natural manner, for there would be two miracles involved in the former case and only one in the latter.

Such, then, are Scotus's thoughts on eucharistic presence and on multiple local presence. Clearly, much of what he says in favor of both is based upon a developing Franciscan tradition. Like many others, he turns to Hugh of St. Victor for support. Like others, he rests his case upon divine omnipotence, utilizing several arguments already familiar to theologians in his order. He is hardly the first to argue that, if God can make two bodies exist in the same place, he can make the same body exist in two places; nor is he original in hypothesizing a situation in which dimension is converted into dimension just as substance is converted into substance.

---

[30] *Op. Oxon.,* IV, d. 10, q. 3, 527–31. See also *Rep. Par.,* IV, d. 10, q. 3, 644f.

His refutation of the arguments against multiple local presence cannot fail to strike a familiar chord, not only because he refutes the same series of arguments already attacked by his predecessors, but also because he often refutes them in much the same way. Note, for example, his appeal to the distinction between absolute and relative properties in order to avoid the specter of contradictory qualities; his acknowledgment that some type of *mutatio* can and must be allowed; and his insistence that ubiquity is possible, although not in the sense that God is ubiquitous.

Scotus is equally dependent upon Franciscan tradition in arguing that conversion is not the formal cause of Christ's presence. In order to establish that fact, one need only trace the pedigree of his resolute distinction between "being" and "being present"; his suggestion that, if conversion should lead to presence anywhere, it would be more likely to lead to presence in heaven than on the altar; and his argument that, if present conversion were the cause, Christ would not remain present after the conversion had taken place.

When one asks precisely which of the theologians already considered Scotus most resembles in utilizing these arguments, an interesting fact emerges. Some of the arguments can be traced to a variety of scholars, thus linking Scotus with William of Ware, William de la Mare, Peter John Olivi, John Pecham and Richard of Middleton. Scotus parallels John Pecham in four cases and Richard of Middleton in five. De la Mare, Olivi and Ware are less in evidence, and Ware explicitly refutes two of the arguments adopted by Scotus. The most striking parallel is with none of these scholars, however, but with Vitalis de Furno. Seven of the nine arguments cited above are used by Vitalis as well as by Duns.

At other points, Scotus's link with the tradition is weaker. He is hardly in the main stream of Franciscan tradition when he argues that transubstantiation simply adds new problems rather than solving the old ones; yet there are precedents in Pecham and Olivi, and Ware expresses some bewilderment on this matter. His positive formulation of eucharistic presence in terms of *respectus extrinsecus adveniens* represents an original contribution; yet even here one can find anticipations, albeit vague ones, in Olivi and Richard, who speak of presence as a *respectus* or *relatio*.

Nevertheless, despite Scotus's debt to the Franciscan tradition, his positive formulation is very much his own. Reinhold Seeberg comments that the basic presupposition of Scotus's argument is his realistic understanding of place, which enables him to separate it from the substance in question.[31] If one means by "place" that containing thing to which the located substance is related, then Scotus's view is not strikingly different from that held by other scholastics. If, however, one takes Seeberg to mean "place" in the sense of "being in a place," then he is quite correct. Duns Scotus's

---

[31] *Duns Scotus*, p. 373. See also his *Lehrbuch der Dogmengeschichte*, 3: 526f.

view of a *respectus extrinsecus adveniens* might be called "realistic" inasmuch as he sees it as capable of being absent even though the two *termini* of the *respectus* are present. Thus a body can coexist with a *locus* without being related to it by any particular *respectus* of *positio* in the predicamental sense. Scotus's understanding of presence as such a *respectus extrinsecus adveniens,* coupled with his view of substance as prior to any such *respectus,* are absolutely central for his formulation of eucharistic presence, and any misrepresentation of these ideas can only lead to a distorted interpretation of his thought.

Oddly enough, Seeberg himself is probably a case in point. He continually represents Scotus as one who has reduced the bodily presence of Christ in the eucharist to a *mere* relation.[32] Again, he tends to think of the distinction between Christ's sacramental presence and his presence in other places as one between the sacramental and the *real* Christ.[33] Once one takes Duns's view of presence seriously, however, it becomes apparent that Christ's presence in the eucharist is just as real as his or anyone else's presence in any other place. Christ may be present in the eucharist "only" by a *respectus extrinsecus adveniens,* but it is also "only" by such a *respectus* that the Statue of Liberty is present in New York harbor.

Whatever may be said of the *respectus extrinsecus adveniens,* it is clear that Scotus works it out in such a way as to erase any necessary connection between eucharistic presence and transubstantiation. God could not only make a body be sacramentally present in several places without substantial conversion, but even effect multiple local presence without such conversion. In fact, as Scotus emphasizes on several occasions, transubstantiation does not in itself furnish an adequate explanation of Christ's presence, since the term of substantial conversion is a new substance, not the presence of that substance in a given place.

With these thoughts in mind, we turn to the Scotus's *ex professo* treatment of conversion in *distinctio* 11 of the *Opus Oxoniense.* He begins with two relatively harmless questions regarding the possibility of transubstantiation, then asks whether the bread is actually converted into the body of Christ.[34] Here some of the most striking features of his view begin to emerge. He begins by citing three opinions on the subject which he describes as those listed by Innocent III: (1) that the bread remains and the body of Christ is present with it; (2) that the bread is not converted, but ceases to exist through annihilation, resolution into matter, or change into another thing (*corruptionem in aliud*); and (3) that the bread and wine are transubstantiated into the body and blood of Christ. All of these opinions, Scotus says, wish to maintain the real presence of Christ's body and blood, since such an affirmation is demanded by faith.

---

[32] See *Duns Scotus,* 376, where it is called "nur eine logische Beziehung." See also ibid., 374f., 383.

[33] See ibid., 374f.

[34] *Op. Oxon.,* IV, d. 11, q. 3, 605–57.

He then turns to a long and tightly packed discussion of the arguments
for each position, beginning with the first. These arguments are so important
for the present study that they must be described in some detail.

The first argument for the permanence of the bread is based upon the
principle of parsimony. No explanation of any phenomenon should in-
troduce more factors than are necessary for the understanding of that
phenomenon. If event X can be explained by positing causes A, B and C,
one should not throw in D and E for good measure. Such a rule, Scotus
suggests,[35] applies to theological as well as philosophical matters. Thus
one must ask how essential a role transubstantiation plays in the explanation
of Christ's real presence.

Here two factors seem to militate against transubstantiation. First, it is
clearly unnecessary for Christ's presence since, as Scotus has already agreed
in *distinctio* 10, the body of Christ could be present along with the bread
and wine. Thus transubstantiation simply adds an additional miracle without contributing anything necessary for the presence itself.[36] Second, conversion is unnecessary for the symbolic aspect of the eucharist, since the
substance of bread, far from ruining the signification of the species by its
presence, would actually be a better sign of Christ's body than the accidents
themselves.[37]

Again, "this way of understanding the real presence [i.e. transubstan-
tiation], which is harder to understand and seems to lead to more contradictions (*inconvenientia*), does not seem to have been handed down to
us as an article of faith."

Again, in matters of faith, "that explanation should not be chosen which
is harder to understand and from which more contradictions seem to
follow"; yet the idea of the bread ceasing to exist "seems harder to defend,
and many more contradictions follow from it, than the idea that the bread
remains." If a position which seems to involve contradictions is touted as
part of the faith, it will alienate "all philosophers, and even all those
following natural reason," from Christianity. It seems, Scotus suggests,
that

a philosopher, or anyone following natural reason, would see a greater contradiction
in this negation of bread than in all the articles of faith concerning the incarnation.
And it seems strange that concerning one article, which is not even a principal
article of faith, something should be asserted which lays the faith open to the
contempt of all those following natural reason.[38]

---

[35] It must be remembered that Scotus is speaking in the person of an anonymous exponent
of the first view, not expressly for himself. The nature of Scotus's own view will be discussed
later.

[36] The principle of parsimony extends to miracles: . . . ponenda sunt pauciora miracula
quantum possibile est."

[37] Note that this argument, like the others in this section, opposes a recognizably Thomistic
argument.

[38] Ibid., pp. 605f.: Secundo sic, et quasi in idem redit, in creditis nobis secundum intellectum
universalem traditis, non videtur ille modus determinandus, qui est difficilior ad intelligandum,
et ad quem plura videntur sequi inconvenientia; sed istud, corpus Christi esse in eucharistia,

Scotus does not enumerate the difficulties involved in the idea of transubstantiation at this time, and we are left to assume that they are the same ones confronted later when he takes up the cudgel for that doctrine.

Again, "nothing is to be held as part of the substance of faith except what is expressly found in the scripture or expressly declared by the church or evidently follows from something plainly contained in the scripture or determined by the church."[39] None of these sources of authority seems to require belief that the substance of bread is absent. If it is argued, "as one doctor says," that the words *hoc est corpus meum* demand the assertion that the substance of bread does not remain, one might respond that, given the permanence of the bread, the phrase could easily mean "this entity contained under this sensible sign is my body," just as it does if we grant the truth of transubstantiation, since, even if such is granted, the *hoc* cannot refer to *all* that is present on the altar but must somehow exclude the accidents of the bread.

Finally, the sacrament of truth should contain no falsity. Accidents naturally signify their substance and should do so in the eucharist. If it is objected that they signify the body of Christ, it can be replied that the natural signification should not be altered through the imposition of a new, freely instituted signification when the truth of both significations could be conserved if the substance were to remain.

The case for the second alternative, annihilation, is very cursorily presented by Scotus. He points out that the first three arguments already cited in favor of the first opinion can also be adduced to prove the superiority of annihilation over transubstantiation as an explanation of the eucharistic presence. That is, it involves less miracles and less *inconvenientia* while seeming equally permissible in the light of scripture and tradition.

Having thus set forth the arguments for the first two opinions, Scotus proceeds to refute the counter-arguments advanced against them by "a certain doctor."[40] In response to the objection that the permanence of bread would lead to idolatry, Scotus asserts that in such a case the *latria*

---

est quoddam verum universaliter traditum nobis; iste autem intellectus, quod non sit ibi substantia panis, videtur difficilior ad sustinendum, et ad ipsum sequuntur plura inconvenientia, quam ponendo ibi esse substantiam panis; ergo, etc. Maior probatur, quia ex quo fides nobis data est, ut sit via ad salutem, ita debet ut videtur determinari, et teneri ab ecclesia, sicut magis est idonea ad salutem; sed ponendo intellectum aliquem talem supra modum difficilem, et ad quem manifeste videntur sequi inconvenientia, est occasio avertendi omnes philosophos, imo fere omnes sequentes rationem naturalem, a fide, vel saltem impediendi eos, ne convertantur ad fidem, si dicatur eis talia pertinere ad fidem nostram; imo videtur, quod philosophus haberet pro maiori inconveniente, vel quicumque sequens naturalem rationem, ea quae ponuntur hic, negando substantiam panis, quam haberet de omnibus articulis, quos habemus de incarnatione. Et mirum videtur, quare in uno articulo, qui non est principalis articulus fidei, debeat talis intellectus asseri, propter quem fides pateat contemptui omnium sequentium rationem.

[39] Ibid., 606: Nihil est tenendum tanquam de substantia fidei, nisi quod potest expresse haberi de scriptura vel expresse declaratum est per ecclesiam, vel evidenter sequitur ex aliquo plane contento in scriptura vel plane determinato ab ecclesia.

[40] Ibid., 607f. These arguments are the same ones advanced by Aquinas in IV *Sent.*, d. 11, q. 1, art. 1.

allotted to the sacrament would be directed toward the body of Christ contained in the bread rather than toward the bread itself, just as it is now directed toward the body of Christ contained under the accidents rather than toward the accidents themselves. Here again Scotus has managed to show that the Thomistic arguments can be turned against the Thomistic formulation. In response to the objection that such permanence would ruin the signification of the sacraments, Scotus repeats what he has already said on this score. In response to the objection that it would detract from the function of the sacrament as spiritual food, making it corporeal food, Scotus observes that it *is* corporeal as well as spiritual food, citing St. Paul's testimony in I *Corinthians* 11 as proof of this fact. Against the objection that Christ cannot become present in the eucharist except through substantial conversion, Scotus simply cites his own argument in *distinctio* 10, *quaestio* 1. In response to the objection that, given such permanence, the biblical text should read *hic est corpus meum* rather than *hoc est corpus meum*, Scotus again raises the spectre of the same problem within the objector's own formulation.

Duns then turns to examine the same doctor's arguments against annihilation. That doctor is represented as arguing that, if the substance of bread were resolved into matter, it would become either pure matter (*materiam nudam*) or matter with some other form. The first would be impossible, since, given the existence of matter without form, the "act of matter" (*actus materiae*) would simultaneously be and not be. In the second case, the resultant new substance would either be present in the same place as the body of Christ or be moved to a different location, both of which are *inconveniens*. Scotus replies that the argument against reduction to *materiam nudam* depends upon an equivocal use of the word *actus*, since it refers in one sense to that "difference of being" (*differentia entis*) opposed to *potentia*, whereas in the second sense it refers to that *habitudo* which form has to the informable. The argument is based upon an equally equivocal use of *potentia*. As opposed to *actus* in the first sense it refers to a being which is diminished (*diminutum*) in its being, being less complete (*completum*) than an *ens in actu*. As opposed to *actus* in the second sense it refers to a principle receptive of an *actus* in the second sense. Thus matter, after being created by God but before being informed, would be *in actu* in the first sense and *in potentia* in the second. In defense of the second possibility, that of the bread being reduced to matter under a new form, Scotus argues that there is no more contradiction involved in the coexistence of the new substance with the body of Christ than in the coexistence of the body of Christ with the quantity of bread, since *quantum* is more repugnant to *quantum* than substance to substance. Nor, on the other hand, has it been demonstrated that it is impossible for God to move the new substance to another place. Thus all three possibilities are defensible.

Scotus has finally finished his presentation of the first two opinions. It is hardly necessary to observe that this presentation represents a conscious effort to refute both chapter and verse of the argument that transubstantiation is necessarily linked with eucharistic presence. Having thus demolished the argument, however, Scotus must still deal with the thesis which the argument was designed to support. At this point he must stand with his opponents and assert the truth of transubstantiation, not for their reasons, but because it is commonly held and *principaliter* because it is held by the holy Roman Church. Although Duns cites Ambrose and provides a brief indication of two points at which the belief is "congruent" with established church practices, he makes it quite clear that the authority of the Roman Church is the crucial factor in his decision.

What, then, of the arguments for the first two opinions? Scotus observes that the principle of parsimony is valid, but that it does not militate against transubstantiation, since it is necessary to posit transubstantiation in order to preserve "the truth of the eucharist" (*veritas Eucharistiae*). Had God instituted the eucharist in such a way as to make the body of Christ coexist with the substance of bread, the *veritas Eucharistiae* could have been saved without positing transubstantiation. Since he did not do so, however, the situation is entirely different.

One is tempted to see in Scotus's response a somewhat superficial bow to churchly authority, less impressive than the original argument; yet such a response may simply betray the degree to which Duns's attitude toward doctrine differs from our own. At any rate, there is more to his response than first meets the eye. In stating implicitly that God's actions are not in themselves governed by the principle of parsimony, he provides a clarification which is of more than passing interest when seen in the context of the age in which he was writing. The opposite notion was hardly untenable in the early fourteenth century.[41] It would, in fact, be hard to avoid if the role of God's reason were emphasized at the expense of his will. Scotus's response places a check upon this sort of thought by stressing God's freedom in regard to the created order. He *could have* done it in one way if he had chosen, but he chose to do it in quite another way.

The reverse side of the same coin might be said to contain an important warning for theologians. If emphasis upon the contingency of the divinely instituted order involves greater attention to divine freedom, it also involves greater awareness of the limitations imposed upon rational argument in theology. Here caution is necessary. Scotus is not advocating a new irrationality. In fact, it is possible to judge from what has been said that his theology is more rational than Thomas's inasmuch as it is based upon a more penetrating analysis of the extent to which theology can be supported by natural reason. The argument for the necessity of transubstantiation is rejected, not because it is rational, but because it is not rationally convincing. It does not prove what it claims to prove.

Thus two different factors would seem to coalesce in the formation of

---

[41] See M. de Gandillac in *Histoire de l'Eglise*, 13: *Le Mouvement doctrinal de XI au XIV siècle*, 373.

Scotus's more "positivistic"[42] approach. On the one hand, emphasis upon divine freedom leads to emphasis upon the contingency of the divinely instituted order, which in turn leads to greater emphasis upon revelation as opposed to natural theology. On the other hand, a critical evaluation of the "proofs" provided by previous theologians leads to a greater awareness of the insufficiency of these "proofs," which in turn leads to a similar emphasis upon revelation as opposed to natural theology. Thus the theologian is encouraged to place more and more reliance upon authoritative revelation concerning the divinely instituted order. If that revelation can be supported by rational arguments, such support is to be welcomed; yet the theologian is made suspicious of such arguments both by theoretical considerations concerning the divine freedom and by his own empirical observation that many arguments have hitherto been proved inconclusive.

The same general attitude is manifested in Scotus's reply to the second argument. All other things being equal, one should not accept the explanation which is more difficult to believe. Nevertheless, such a rule cannot be used to refute what we know to be the truth.[43] Here again one is tempted to protest that Duns the philosopher has been betrayed by Duns the churchman. Here again, however, such an evaluation would be premature. Once a theologian is aware of the extent to which natural theology falls short in its construction of rational proofs for Christian doctrine, he should be equally skeptical concerning any attempt to construct a rational disproof of some doctrine. Such an attitude need not result in a precipitous flight from rationality. It could just as easily result in a rational awareness of the limits inherent in human thought and a healthy distrust of any rational argument which concerns matters lying at the fringe of our understanding. So far Scotus's admonition is open to the latter interpretation. Whether such an interpretation can be maintained throughout his discussion of eucharistic conversion can only be decided after viewing the entire discussion.

It is noteworthy that Scotus's responses to the first two arguments contain explicit reference to an authoritatively revealed truth which counterbalances the claims of any strictly rational argument. Thus both of these responses anticipate his response to the third argument, that regarding authority. Here Scotus reveals the precise source of the truth which he is defending. It is, of course, the Fourth Lateran Council.[44] Opposing arguments regarding the Bible and early tradition are true as far as they go. Neither the Bible nor the early church presents an explicit doctrine of transubstantiation. Nevertheless, this question has been settled once and for all by the decree of the Fourth Lateran Council, "in which the truth of some things to be believed is set out more explicitly than in the Apostles', Athanasian and Nicene creeds."

---

[42] See Seeberg, *Duns Scotus,* 381.
[43] IV *Sent.,* d. 11, q. 3, 618.
[44] Ibid: Ecclesia declaravit istum intellectum esse de veritate fidei in illo symbolo edito sub Innoc. tertio in concilio Lateranensi Firmitur credimus etc.

Thus Scotus's formulation of the doctrine is striking, not only in its refusal to offer rational justification for the doctrine, but also in its apparent willingness to base the doctrine upon the decision of a council less than a century old in his day, a decision admittedly based upon no clear-cut biblical or patristic precedents. On what basis, then, could the church have arrived at "such a difficult interpretation of this article," especially "when the words of scripture would support an easy and apparently truer interpretation"?[45] Scotus's answer is that in choosing this interpretation the church was guided by the same spirit through which the scriptures were written and handed down. Thus it chose the true interpretation.[46]

Such a view demands a new look at what Duns has to say about the scriptural authority for transubstantiation. As Antonius Vellico rightly suggests,[47] Scotus is not placing the Fourth Lateran Council alongside the Bible as an independent authority. On the contrary, the Council was interpreting scripture when it demanded belief in transubstantiation. No matter how vaguely scripture may have put the matter, its true meaning is now clear.

Such an explanation tells us everything and nothing. It clearly states the conciliar claim to doctrinal authority, yet it says absolutely nothing about the sorts of criteria which would enter into the doctrinal decision. Granting that the bishops at the Council were guided by the Holy Spirit, their interpretation must have been based on some concrete evidence. What evidence does Scotus think was decisive? This question must, unfortunately, remain unanswered, since there is nothing in his formulation which would help us to answer it.

So far, we have examined Scotus's presentation and refutation of the arguments for the first two opinions and his assertion that the third opinion, transubstantiation, is the correct one. He must also show in good scholastic fashion that it is possible, that it is not a contradictory notion in itself nor does it lead to such. It is in these sections that one would expect him to come to terms with the *inconvenientia* seemingly entailed by the doctrine, and it is in the context of this confrontation that one might expect to discover what Duns really means by "transubstantiation."

The first stage of this confrontation actually takes place with his answer to the question "whether transubstantiation is possible."[48] Here, having

---

[45] Ibid., Et si queras quare voluit ecclesia eligere istum intellectum ita difficilem huius articuli, cum verba scripturae possent salvari secundum intellectum facilem, et veriorem secundum apparentiam de hoc articulo . . .

[46] Ibid., Dico quod eo spiritu expositae sunt scripturae quo conditae. Et ita supponendum est, quod ecclesia catholica eo spiritu exposuit, quo tradita est nobis fides. Spiritu scilicet veritatis edocta, et ideo hunc intellectum eligit, quia verus est. Non enim in potestate ecclesiae fuit facere istud verum vel non verum, sed Dei instituentis, sed intellectum a Deo traditum ecclesia explicavit directa in hoc ut creditur spiritu veritatis.

[47] "De transsubstantiatione iuxta Ioannem Duns Scotum," 308. For a recent investigation of Scotus' views on the relation of tradition and scripture, see Eligius Buytaert, "Circa doctrinam Duns Scoti de traditione et de Scripturae sufficientia adnotationes," 346–62.

[48] Ibid., d. 11, q. k, 585–95.

defined transubstantiation as "the total transition of a substance into a substance,"[49] he argues that "it is not repugnant for whatever is able to be entirely new to succeed that which is able to cease to be entirely . . . consequently this is able to be converted totally into that and thus transubstantiated."[50] Whatever may be the merits of such an explanation, it is obvious that it does not support the possibility of transubstantiation in the sense in which Thomas Aquinas would want to use the word. What it does support is the possibility of a succession of being or, more precisely, of the ceasing-to-be of one thing to the beginning-to-be of another. This apparent insufficiency represents something more than an oversight of Scotus's part, as will be seen in a moment.

Even a casual reading of Scotus's explanation seems to uncover a major fallacy. It seems to apply to any situation except the one to which he intended it to apply, since the body of Christ, being preexistent, is not really produced *de novo* in the eucharistic conversion. Here the striking dissimilarity between Scotus and Aquinas is again demonstrated. Whereas, for the latter, Christ's preexistence is an important part of the argument for the necessity of transubstantiation, for the former it seems one of the gravest threats to the same doctrine.

Scotus replies that two modes of transubstantiation must be distinguished. In the first, the substance takes on being (*esse*). In the second, it takes on "being-here" (*esse hic*).[51] The first is productive (*productiva*) of its term, the second adductive (*adductiva*). The first mode of transubstantiation cannot have a preexistent substance as its term, but the second can. The sort of transubstantiation involved in the eucharistic conversion is, then, of the second type.

Scotus immediately acknowledges the inevitable objection to this line of thought: The second type is not transubstantiation at all, since its term is not substance in itself but presence, which is an accident of substance. He replies that substance is indeed the term of transubstantiation in the second sense, since substance succeeds substance.[52] Such an argument would not seem to be completely at odds with the Thomistic view. It simply focuses attention on the area in which the concept of transubstantiation is relevant. The concept refers, not to the mutation which occurs in Christ (which involves change of presence rather than change of substance), but to the change which occurs upon the altar. The latter does involve a change of substance. This rather obvious affirmation is the only one Duns needs in order to make his point. His argument requires a quiet

---

[49] Ibid.: . . . transitio totalis substantiae in substantiam . . .

[50] Ibid.: Quicquid potest esse totaliter novum non repugnat sibi succedere alii, quod potest totaliter desinere esse . . . et per consequens hoc potest converti totaliter in illam, et ita transubstantiari.

[51] Ibid., d. 11, q. 3, 626.

[52] Ibid.: . . . substantia est terminus ipsius transsubstantiationis secundo modo dictae, quia ipsa substantia succedit substantiae, non tamen habet esse substantiale novum, sed tantum praesentiam novam.

revision of his earlier distinction between transubstantiation and presence,[53] but once this revision is made his defense of transubstantiation is assured, provided that the word is not taken to mean anything more than a succession of substance to substance.

Unfortunately, the term was assumed to mean something more in the later thirteenth century. Transubstantiation meant conversion, and conversion meant more for Thomas, Bonaventure and others than simple succession. At least a minimum degree of assent to this view was exacted through the practice of answering in the negative the question of whether the bread is annihilated in the conversion. For a theologian like Thomas, the "strong" sense of transubstantiation is so obvious and so necessary for his understanding of eucharistic presence that the question of annihilation hardly needs to be asked. For Scotus, the situation is entirely reversed. His understanding of presence and his definition of transubstantiation are such that one eagerly turns to his consideration of the question of annihilation, half expecting him to answer in the affirmative.

The expectation is not completely unfulfilled. Scotus's treatment of this question is a strange one.[54] After beginning, according to his usual pattern, with the presentation and refutation of various opposing arguments, Scotus makes an explicit statement "that the bread is not annihilated, or at least that the bread is not annihilated by this conversion";[55] yet his determination, rather than taking the form of a sustained argument, might almost be termed a monologue. At times one gets the impression that Scotus is thinking out loud.[56] Within this section one can isolate at least four answers to the problem. The first three are immediately followed by refutations. The fourth provides the traditional negation, but in as minimal a form as one could expect to encounter. The conversion is between the bread as present and the body of Christ as present. Thus, within this conversion, the bread does not lose "being-in-itself" (*esse simpliciter*) but only "being-here" (*hic esse*). What, then, do we make of the fact that the bread ceases to *be* as well as to *be present*? This phenomenon must come about through a different act than that involved in transubstantiation.[57] This "ceasing-to-be," although concomitant with the conversion, is not a term of the conversion.[58] Thus, even though this "ceasing-to-be" might be described

---

[53] Duns now says that his distinction, employed with gusto against the Thomistic opinion in d. 10, q. 1, applies only to the first mode of transubstantiation.

[54] Ibid., d. 11, 9. 4, 657–72.

[55] Ibid., d. 11, q. 4, 660: . . . quod panis non annihilatur, vel quod est facilius, quod panis ista conversione non annihilatur.

[56] In view of the arrangement of the arguments in this quaestio and the relation of some of these arguments to those used by Scotus himself in *Quodl.*, q. 10, and the *Reportata Parisiensia*, liber IV, d. 11, q. 4, it is tempting to see the discussion of the *Opus Oxoniense* as a relatively late formulation incorporating former views, later refinements of these views and the final solution of the question in the light of the distinction between productive and adductive transubstantiation.

[57] IV *Sent.*, d. 11, q. 4, 667: . . . oportet quod desinat esse alia desitione, quae est a simpliciter esse eius ad simpliciter non esse eius . . .

[58] Ibid.: . . . illud autem non esse eius, licet quasi concomitetur praesentiam corporis, ut hic, non tamen ut terminum eiusdem generis . . .

as annihilation, the conversion is not thereby implicated.[59] Returning for
a moment to the assertion with which Scotus began his determination,
we see that he has succeeded in backing at least the second of his two
claims. The bread is not annihilated *by the conversion*.[60]

What is one to make of this conclusion? It is of course impossible to
agree with one of his more extreme defenders that Scotus is in complete
agreement with St. Thomas on the matter.[61] On the other end of the
spectrum, it is equally impossible to accept Seeberg's attempt to present
Scotus's theory of adductive transubstantiation as essentially a doctrine
of consubstantiation phrased in accordance with the demands of orthodoxy.[62] There is no compelling reason to believe that Duns' initial case
for the permanence of the bread represents his own secret opinion or that
it is the only opinion consistent with his view of eucharistic presence. It
is noteworthy that the most striking aspect of that case, his reference to
the ridicule heaped upon transubstantiation by those following natural
reason, argues *against* transubstantiation rather than *for* consubstantiation.
Again, one must not fail to note that the most forceful arguments advanced
by Duns Scotus in favor of the permanence of the bread are also listed
by him as valid arguments for the superiority of an annihilation theory
over that of transubstantiation. In other words, although it is true that the
permanence theory is supported with one more argument than is accorded
to the annihilation theory, the main point of the opening section is not
so much the superiority of one of those views to the other as the superiority
of both to transubstantiation.

Furthermore, if we are to take seriously the rebuttals of these opening
arguments offered by Scotus himself—rebuttals which, in their emphasis
upon divine freedom and the centrality of revealed truth, accord well with
Scotus's views elsewhere—we must recognize that he would not accept
as decisive any slight rational superiority on the part of a given theory.
Thus, as we noted earlier, the real problem is one of how prodigious the
difficulties accompanying transubstantiation actually seem. Scotus might
be expected to find transubstantiation a major stumbling block only if the
inconvenientia seem so unassailable as to involve any formulation in hope-
less self-contradiction.

Once we examine Scotus's own formulation in the light of these considerations, we might be moved to conclude that he is, in fact, unable to
formulate a thoroughgoing doctrine of transubstantiation in the "strong"
Thomistic sense of that word. Is there anything especially sinister about
this conclusion? In the long run, one would guess that there is not, even

---

[59] Ibid.: . . . et per consequens si ista desitio secundum se considerata sit annihilatio, tamen
nullo modo ista conversio est annihilatio.

[60] He explicitly recognizes this fact. Ibid., 666: Potest ergo teneri tertium scilicet secundum
membrum disiunctivae positae supra.

[61] Hugolinus Storff, *De natura transubstantiationis iuxta I. Duns Scotum*, 74.

[62] See *Lehrbuch der Dogmengeschichte*, 3, 522f.; *Duns Scotus*, 382f., 386f., 393f.

if we choose to measure Scotus by the canons of Roman Catholic doctrine. His view of transubstantiation is not explicitly contradicted by the definition of transubstantiation produced by the Council of Trent, nor did the great theologians of the sixteenth and seventeenth centuries interpret the Tridentine definition as a condemnation of Scotus.[63]

In the short run, the situation is more ambiguous. Scotus himself may well have felt somewhat uncomfortable about his position. He seems to see himself as moving in a tradition which clearly expects a negative answer to the question of "whether the bread is annihilated." He states the problem in such a way as to demand such an answer, since he introduces the theory of annihilation as an alternative to transubstantiation. He eventually escapes from his dilemma through an artful application of the two theories to different phenomena. As the discussion ends, one senses an atmosphere of relief rather than exultation.

Scotus's solution to the problem in the *Reportata Parisiensia* is strikingly different.[64] There he affirms that the bread is not annihilated because the *terminus ad quem* of annihilation is absolutely nothing, whereas that of conversion is Christ's body. He then launches an objection against this view and, in the process of answering the objection, states that in eucharistic conversion there are not two changes with four terms, as in the case of corruption and generation, but only one change with two positive terms.[65]

If, on the other hand, one should argue that transubstantiation involves two changes—one from the being of bread to its nonbeing, the other from the nonbeing of the bread to Christ's being—"then it would be harder to respond." Nevertheless, it can be argued that annihilation of the bread still would not follow, for transubstantiation does not lead to negation *extra genus*, due to the fact that there is a positive term, even though there is no common subject. Thus one would say that, if air were converted into fire, even if there were no common matter, the air would not be annihilated, since it was converted into a positive term.

If Scotus considered such an argument valid at the turn of the fourteenth century, he certainly did not continue to think of it as such. In a quodlibetal question dating from 1306 to 1307,[66] Scotus includes this argument among those which he refutes, insisting that, if there are two positive terms, then there must be two negative ones as well.

Here Scotus attempts a different sort of explanation. In the case of natural corruption, there is not an absolute annihilation but rather a negation or privation of the form in something which has an aptitude for form. In the case of transubstantiation, the lack of any common matter rules out any such "aptitude," yet the destruction of the bread is still not a negation

---

[63] See Vellico, "De transsubstantiatione," 323–31.

[64] *Rep. Par.*, d. 11, q. 4, 673–76.

[65] *Rep. Par.*, 675.

[66] *Quaestiones quodlibetales*, St. Bonaventure, Franciscan Institute, 1950, q. 10, a. 3.

which rules out everything, but one included in the being of the positive *terminus ad quem.*

In the *Opus Oxoniense,*[67] the solution of the *Reportata Parisiensia* is again considered and dismissed. The solution of the quodlibetal question is also cited and becomes the starting point of a long series of considerations leading ultimately to his final conclusion. Thus, on the matter of annihilation, the *Opus Oxoniense* does seem to support Charles Balić's admonition that, "whenever disagreement exists between the teaching of the *Ordinatio* and the teaching of the *Reportationes,* the text of the *Ordinatio* is to be followed as that which reflects Scotus's final and definitive doctrine."[68] In this case, the status of the *Ordinatio* as "final and definitive" doctrine might be defended, not only against the *Reportationes,* but against the quodlibetal questions as well. Perhaps "final" is more apt than "definitive," however, since Scotus's thoughts on the subject of annihilation seem to have been the process of development during the last few years of his life and might well have continued to change had he not died in 1308.

---

[67] *Op. Oxon.,* d. 11, q. 4, 661–66.
[68] Charles Balić, "Life and Works," 21.

VIII. CONCLUSION

We are now in a position to summarize our findings and make a few general observations. First, by the time of John Pecham, Franciscan theologians who wrestled with the doctrine of eucharistic presence could take advantage of an impressive formulation of that doctrine which we have labeled the Thomist-Bonaventuran thesis. According to that thesis, the doctrine of transubstantiation offered both an adequate and a necessary explanation of eucharistic presence. It was an adequate explanation in the sense that transubstantiation was seen as the cause of Christ's presence. He was there precisely because the bread and wine were converted into his body and blood.

According to the Thomist-Bonaventuran thesis, transubstantiation accounted, not only for Christ's presence, but also for the nature of his presence. After all, there was much to be accounted for. Christ was not simply present in the church as the priest was present there. He was present in several churches at once as well as in heaven, and he was present in these churches in such a way that he could not be seen, touched, tasted, or harmed in any way. How could that be?

The answer seemed to lie in the fact that transubstantiation meant conversion of one substance into another. Only the substance of Christ's body and blood was thus present through the conversion. The rest—his soul, divinity and accidents—were present by concomitance. Thus, to use the happy terminology developed by Thomas Aquinas, everything was present in the manner of substance, which is totally present in each part, rather than through the mediation of dimensions.

For the Thomistic-Bonaventuran thesis, transubstantiation was also a necessary explanation. If the bread and wine were not converted into Christ's body and blood, then eucharistic presence would be impossible. Annihilation and consubstantiation could be eliminated, not only by appeal to authority and church practices, but also on the basis of sheer reason. Multiple presence could be achieved only through substantial conversion.

The argument was an ingenious one, and it was backed by two scholars so eminent that any modern undergraduate might be expected to recognize their names. To be sure, Thomas and Bonaventure blended with their environment a bit more neatly in the later thirteenth century than that modern undergraduate might realize. The centrality enjoyed by Aquinas in modern history textbooks would only be achieved over the centuries, with the aid of Dante, John XXII, Leo XIII, and a host of others. Nevertheless, even in 1270, he and Bonaventure had a good deal of clout. Any theologian who found himself perplexed by the enigma of eucharistic presence might understandably be grateful for such an excellent theory by such famous scholars.

Thus it is all the more notable that a whole series of Franciscan scholars turned their backs on the Thomist-Bonaventuran thesis and struck out on an entirely different course. Their reasons for doing so are, as we have seen, incredibly complex, but certain basic tendencies are hard to miss. In the first place, almost all the theologians who argue against the Thomist-Bonaventuran thesis cite Hugh of St. Victor. This fact is noteworthy, but perhaps it can be misleading. There is no reason to assume that the thesis was regretfully discarded because it did not square with a respected authority. On the contrary, it seems more likely that Hugh was pressed into service because these theologians needed a recognized authority for a point they wished to make, just as John of Damascus was recruited to stand as surety for the opposite view.

The passage from Hugh which this group of Franciscan theologians found so richly satisfying was useful to them because it served to anchor their appeal to divine omnipotence. Over and over again, these theologians insist that the Thomist-Bonaventuran thesis, in presenting transubstantiation as a necessary explanation of eucharistic presence, unduly limits the sphere of God's power. In essence, they argue that Christ could be present as he now is present in the eucharist without any conversion, and, bolder still, that Christ or anything else could be locally present in several places without conversion. Granting the degree of unclarity on this matter in the writings of William de la Mare and Matthew of Aquasparta, it is nonetheless true that both propositions are defended in the writings of certain Franciscan theologians from the time of John Pecham on.

To be sure, these theologians do not always adopt a definite stance. John Pecham, Roger Marston and Vitalis de Furno all observe that "wise men differ" on the matter of multiple local presence. Pecham and Marston do not commit themselves, nor does Vitalis always explicitly do so. Nevertheless, the arguments are there in any case, and Vitalis does explicitly accept them on occasion, as do Peter John Olivi, William of Falgar, Richard of Middleton, William of Ware, and John Duns Scotus.

In order to support the claims that God can cause Christ to be present in the eucharist without conversion and that he can make a thing be locally present in several places at once, these theologians had to show that such claims did not involve logical contradiction. They could do so in a positive or negative manner, arguing either that such things were possible or that the standard arguments against their possibility were without force.

On the positive side, one might argue that Christ could be present in the eucharist without conversion because God can produce immediately any effect which he normally produces through a created cause. Again, one might defend either the possibility of eucharistic presence without conversion or the possibility of multiple local presence by citing the existence of phenomena which seem either somehow analogous or at least equally impossible. If God can conserve Christ's body in the eucharist without conversion or make it cease to be present there without conversion, then he can cause it to become present without such. If God can make two bodies exist in the same place, he can make one body simultaneously exist in several places.

On the other hand, one could proceed by envisaging imaginary situations which seem possible and would lead to multiple local presence. Suppose God were to convert dimensions into dimensions, just as he converts substance into substance. Suppose he were to convert various parts of the air, each the size of Christ's body, into his body. Such forays into the world of fantasy often suggest remarkable creative faculties and can by no means be dismissed as the transmogrification of solid, constructive theology into a sterile game. They are directed toward an important goal: A clearer definition of the spheres of divine omnipotence. Such a task, useful in any case, was made particularly necessary by the exhuberant theologizing of the later thirteenth century, which, in its zeal to justify God's ways to man, might be tempted to compromise divine power by offering *rationes* which seemed to bind God to the present order of things. Such a danger was worth guarding against. As Pecham observes, in doubtful cases it is safer to attribute possibility to God than to deny it.

The argument could also be carried on in a negative manner, by refuting the arguments offered by other theologians. In some cases, the answer involved conceding part of the opposing view. Thus a whole series of scholars found themselves countering the objection that, without conversion, the body of Christ would undergo *mutatio*, by arguing that it would undergo such in any case, but that some types of *mutatio* can be accepted by the theologian. As to the objection that multiple local presence would lead to the possibility of ubiquity, Pecham denies that such is the case, while Vitalis and Scotus concede the fact but underline that this ubiquity would not be the same as God's.

The most common gambit in attacking multiple local presence is the insistence that it would involve one in making contradictory statements about Christ's body. He would be hot in Paris and cold in Rome; or equal in size both to each place separately and to all places combined; or outside his own limits. The first sort of objection, the claim of contradictory properties, is countered partly by distinguishing between absolute and relative properties. The second, concerning size, is refuted by arguing that the case is no different than it would be if the same body were in several places successively. The third is answered in different ways. Pecham answers it by distinguishing between the intrinsic limits of a thing and the extrinsic limits dictated by place, Scotus by distinguishing between two different ways in which one set of *termini* can be related to another.

So far we have dealt with those arguments directed toward proving the possibility of multiple presence without conversion. In other words, we have been looking at arguments against the notion that transubstantiation is a necessary explanation of eucharistic presence. We have seen, however, that those scholars who defended the possibility of multiple presence without conversion sometimes took a strikingly different route, one in which they contended that transubstantiation was not the reason for eucharistic presence in any case. In short, in the process of attacking the idea of transubstantiation as a necessary explanation of eucharistic presence, they disputed its status as an adequate explanation.

Their arguments to this end are varied, but three basic ones can be isolated. First, a number of these theologians draw a sharp distinction between "being" and "being present." Substantial conversion relates to the former, not the latter. As Scotus neatly puts it, substance is the *per se terminus ad quem* of transubstantiation, and nothing posterior to the *per se terminus ad quem* can be the result of transubstantiation. Olivi is equally succinct in stating that acceptance of transubstantiation as the cause of eucharistic presence would entail identifying Christ's body with its presence.

In other words, the relationship between conversion and presence under a particular species of bread and wine is, in good scholastic terms, entirely accidental. Thus conversion would not necessarily lead to presence under one particular set of accidents rather than another set.

Several scholars, while denying the connection between substantial conversion and presence, also argue that, if there were such a connection, then the converted bread would be more likely to acquire presence in heaven than on the altar. As Scotus says, what is converted into a preexistent thing is more apt to acquire the conditions of that thing than the reverse. William of Ware explicitly divorces himself from this argument, but other scholars like William de la Mare and Vitalis de Furno espouse it.

A third mode of attack probes the difficulties raised by the fact that the conversion is a transitory act which does not coexist in time with Christ's presence. If presence were causally connected with conversion as taking place, then it would last only as long as the conversion does. If, on the other hand, presence were causally connected with conversion as having taken place, it is hard to see how such a presence would be terminated with the destruction of the eucharistic species.

Having thus reviewed the nature of the attack, we should also pause for a moment to determine its limits. As we have seen, William de la Mare and Matthew of Acquasparta present an ambiguous picture. William denies in one work that eucharistic presence demands transubstantiation, yet another work which may be by William seems to combine such a denial with an argument against annihilation which assumes that transubstantiation is a necessary explanation of eucharistic presence. Matthew, in two separate questions, both affirms and denies the possibility of multiple local presence.

Pecham is ambiguous in another sense. He affirms that Christ could be present in the sacrament without transubstantiation, yet he takes no stand on the issue of multiple local presence, simply commenting that "wise men contradict wise men" and listing the arguments and counterarguments for both positions. Roger Marston follows him in seeing the latter question as an open one. Vitalis de Furno, in one question, follows Pecham and

Marston in noting that "wise men contradict wise men" on the issue and in failing to state any definite opinion of his own; yet he gives most of his attention to the arguments in favor of multiple local presence and in another question he explicitly accepts that possibility.

Thus only Peter Olivi, William of Falgar, Richard of Middleton, William of Ware and Duns Scotus consistently take a position, and even in these cases the position varies somewhat from person to person. All deny that transubstantiation is necessary for eucharistic presence, yet there is some variation as to how presence and transubstantiation should be related. William of Falgar says it is neither final, formal, material nor efficient cause of Christ's presence. Richard of Middleton says transubstantiation is the efficient cause of Christ's presence, but not its final cause. William of Ware says it is not the cause of Christ's presence, but rather of the manner of his presence. Scotus argues that transubstantiation is not the formal cause of eucharistic presence, and his notion of presence is such that it would be difficult to see conversion as any other sort of cause, whether of presence or manner of presence.

The point is worth pondering. Since many scholars before Scotus assume that transubstantiation is at least the cause of Christ's mode of existence in the eucharist, they can utilize various other aspects of the Thomist-Bonaventuran formulation in order to explain why Christ is unseen, untouched, uninjured, etc. Thus Richard, Vitalis and William of Ware can still speak of Christ being present in the manner of substance rather than through the mediation of dimensions. Olivi explicitly rejects the notion of presence in the manner of substance, but even he can talk about concomitance, as indeed does Scotus.

It was, of course, possible to push the criticism of transubstantiation one step further, one step beyond the point necessary to prove that it was not an adequate explanation of presence. One might argue that the idea of transubstantiation not only served no purpose in explaining eucharistic presence but actually created problems of its own. It was thus not merely unhelpful but positively burdensome. Few scholars took this line, but it is interesting to find such an argument at both ends of our chronological period. Both Pecham and Scotus explicitly point to the conceptual difficulties of transubstantiation, while Olivi and Ware also seem to have trouble with the doctrine. Such is hardly surprising. As we will see in a moment, these scholars' examination of eucharistic theology had helped to sharpen a problem regarding transubstantiation which had been recognized outside the Franciscan order as well.

The preceding summary of these Franciscans' assault on transubstantiation as necessary and adequate explanation hardly includes all the arguments offered in that cause, nor does it represent an accurate picture of any particular theologian. It is, rather, a collage assembled to represent the general thrust of their attack, and as such it has limited value.

One cannot examine these scholars without noting the peculiar blend of conservatism and innovation which characterizes their thought on transubstantiation. Some of them, like John Pecham and William de la Mare, are routinely mentioned in connection with the conservative reaction of the 1270s. Olivi, too, is often described as a conservative, although the censure of his works in 1283 adds a new dimension to that designation. At any rate, all of these theologians might be considered conservative to the extent that they reject transubstantiation as a necessary explanation of eucharistic presence because such an idea threatens to compromise divine omnipotence. This seems, to be sure, a rather limited notion of conservatism, but it is worth taking seriously. As modern writers have noted, the condemnation of 1277 was very concerned with the threat to divine omnipotence lurking in the sort of Aristotelianism being bruited about in the Parisian arts faculty. In the eucharistic theology produced by our small band of Franciscans, we find a definite correlative to that concern.

The eucharistic theology produced by them was not anti-Aristotelian in the sense that it arose from a basic rejection of the Stagirite. From the 1260s, we find many Franciscans proclaiming that Aristotle was in some ways not merely wrong but pernicious. Bonaventure, Olivi and others were sufficiently concerned to speak of the menace in apocalyptic terms.[1] Nevertheless, it is clear that even Olivi, who had the nastiest things to say about Aristotle, did not reject his philosophy completely.[2]

Nor was their eucharistic theology anti-Aristotelian in the sense that it resulted from a conscious rejection of specific Aristotelian views. To be sure, some criticisms of Aristotle were expressed along the way, as when Olivi noted that Aristotle's predicaments have no room for eucharistic presence; yet similar criticisms were offered by those who supported the Thomist-Bonaventuran position. Indeed, according to Giles of Rome, the very notion of accidents without a subject contradicts Aristotle.[3]

Nevertheless, even if the attack was not inspired by explicit criticism of Aristotelian views, it was connected with a pervasive anxiety engendered by the contemporary scholastic milieu and closely linked with Aristotle's popularity. The problem was not Aristotelian philosophy itself, but a concomitant of the thirteenth-century Aristotelian "boom," the desire to provide Christian doctrine with as much rational foundation as possible. In their zeal to bolster the credentials of transubstantiation, Bonaventure and Thomas made eucharistic presence depend on it in such a way as to deny God's ability to produce multiple bodily presence in any other fashion. John Pecham's *Questions on the Eucharist*, written well before the condemnation of 1277 and probably around the time of the 1270 condemnation, show that by that date some people were already sufficiently attuned to the problem of divine omnipotence to question the Thomist-Bonaventuran thesis.

---

[1] See Burr, "The Apocalyptic Element in Olivi's Critique of Aristotle," 15–29.
[2] See Orazio Bettini, "Olivi di fronte ad Aristotele," 176–97.
[3] *Errores philosophorum*, pp. 8f. and 12f.

Viewed from this perspective, criticism of their view might be seen as an extension of the very principle which would have led not only Stephen Tempier but Bonaventure and Aquinas themselves to affirm those four articles on the separability of accidents in the 1277 condemnation. Bonaventure, Aquinas and Tempier all denied a necessary link between substance and accident. Pecham denied a necessary link between eucharistic presence and conversion. All acted in the name of divine omnipotence. What God does by means of secondary causes he can do directly. Bonaventure and Aquinas acknowledged this doctrine to the point of accepting accidents without a subject. Pecham invited them to carry their own logic one step further. Pecham's thoughts on the matter, then, can be called anti-Aristotelian only if Aquinas's view is also considered to be such.

If the attack can be termed anti-Aristotelian only in a limited sense, in no sense can it be called anti-intellectual. Franciscan theologians who challenged the Thomist-Bonaventuran thesis did not simply write it off by raising the banners of divine omnipotence and unfathomable mystery. They subjected the thesis to a searching analysis and, in the process, did some serious thinking about the relationship between conversion and presence. Ultimately their cogitations would include some fascinating observations on what is meant by being in a place. Thus one can describe their work, not simply as a "conservative reaction," but rather as a continuing scholarly endeavor which, although partly motivated by the desire to conserve an important element in Christian dogma, went beyond mere conservation to produce important developments in theology.

How positive were those developments? While a full-scale answer to that question would exceed the author's powers and the reader's patience, a few comments may be in order. In the first place, it seems hard to deny that our Franciscan scholars pointed to real weaknesses in the Thomist-Bonaventuran thesis, which was less successful in explaining away the difficulties of eucharistic presence than its originators may have imagined or its adherents claimed. Such a critique is, in itself, an important contribution.

A greater problem arises when we ask what our Franciscans could offer in place of the discredited thesis. Granting that the enigmas of eucharistic presence could not be banished by appealing to transubstantiation, by what alternate means could they be banished? Such a question did not have to be formulated for some time, since, as we have seen, most of these theologians did not entirely abandon transubstantiation as an explanatory principle. Even if they did not accept it as the cause of Christ's presence, they continued to accept it as explaining the manner of his presence. Olivi may have rejected the notion of presence *modo substantiae*, but most of his colleagues did not. Even Olivi was willing to talk about presence through concomitance.

Nevertheless, even from the beginning, certain questions needed to be answered and could not be answered well. For example, the notion of multiple presence brought into focus the problem of what it means to be an individual, a problem reflected in some of the objections to multiple local presence. It is hard to read the answers to these objections with any feeling of relief that a difficult question has been settled. One sometimes feels the authors could argue quite successfully that multiple local presence is no more impossible than multiple sacramental presence, but that is not the same as arguing that either is possible.

It is Scotus who comes closest to offering a satisfactory solution to the problem, at least in the context of his own philosophical presuppositions. It is no accident that he is the only one of our Franciscans recognized as a major scholar. He deserves that recognition. When one examines his analysis of presence in terms of *respectus extrinsicus adveniens* and his application of that concept to the problem of eucharistic presence, one can see why he is known as "the subtle doctor."

Nevertheless, Scotus's explanation could have only a limited currency in his day, since it depended upon a view of *respectus* which was strongly realistic in the medieval philosophical sense. In other words, a thing could be present in one or more places and in one or more ways through a series of *respectus* which could be added or subtracted without any change in either the thing or the places. Such a notion would be philosophical non-sense to Ockham and his followers, and they would have to strike out in a different direction in order to explain eucharistic presence.

If Scotus was at least partly successful in dealing with the issue of eucharistic presence in the context of his own assumptions, he was less so with that of transubstantiation. Here again, his plight was related to the development of thought within our group of Franciscans. We have seen that Scotus has genuine difficulty getting rid of the notion of anni-hilation. He finally succeeds in affirming that the bread is not annihilated, but only by a series of qualifications which seem to let annihilation in through a window after solemnly ejecting it from the front door. Scotus is not alone in this matter. As we have seen, William of Ware only rejects annihilation because, despite his own ratiocinations to the contrary, he elects to hold his "understanding captive and be one with the *sancti*."

Scotus and Ware are, to some extent, wrestling with a problem that plagued any number of people in the later thirteenth century, that of how one can affirm a genuine conversion of one thing into another when, as in the case of transubstantiation, there is no remaining element to unite the two extremes of the conversion. How does such a conversion differ from a simple succession of two things? We have seen that the question bothered men like Henry of Ghent and Godfrey of Fontaines, both of whom generally accepted the Thomist-Bonaventuran thesis.

At the same time, it is tempting to say that the rejection of transub-stantiation as a necessary or adequate explanation of eucharistic presence tended to concentrate attention on the question of conversion versus succession. In the first place, as we have seen, Pecham and Scotus explicitly noted the difficulties of transubstantiation in the course of their attack on the Thomist-Bonaventuran thesis. Second, rejection of the Thomist-Bonaventuran thesis erased a good part of the function of transubstantiation as an explanatory tool in eucharistic theology.

The result was two-fold. On the one hand, the doctrine of transubstantiation became less useful and more a problem to be solved. On the other hand, the existence of transubstantiation could no longer be proved by reference to eucharistic presence. Thomas could argue that the bread must be transubstantiated rather than annihilated because, if it were annihilated, there would be no way for Christ to be present. Once the possibility of presence without conversion was accepted, one had to look for other reasons why transubstantiation must be accepted. Richard of Middleton points to the words *hoc est corpus meum*, the canon of the mass, and eucharistic practices. Scotus rests his case squarely on the Fourth Lateran Council.

The result of this change is that one powerful reason for distinguishing between conversion and annihilation disappeared. Thomas and his followers may have recognized the problem of how to affirm a substantial conversion without any common elements, but they knew that transubstantiation had to differ from annihilation because one of the two could produce eucharistic presence and the other could not. In rejecting transubstantiation as a necessary and adequate explanation, our Franciscans robbed themselves of this neat distinction and thus made it one degree harder to work out an adequate denial of annihilation. Here again, Ockham, who was censured in 1325/26 for using the word "annihilation" in connection with the eucharistic conversion, was an unfortunate heir of this tradition.[4]

---

[4] See Burr, "Ockham, Scotus, and the Censure at Avignon," 144–59.

BIBLIOGRAPHY

ABBREVIATIONS

AFH   *Archivum franciscanum historicum*
FS   *Franziskanische Studien*
LTK   *Lexikon für Theologie und Kirche*
PL   *Patrologiae cursus completus*, series latina

UNPUBLISHED PRIMARY SOURCES

Anonymous, *Quaestiones theologicae*, MS Oxford, Bodl. 859.
Guilelmus de la Mare, *Quodlibeta*, MS Rome, Vat. Borgh. 361.
—— (?), *Super sententias*, MSS Florence, Bibl. Naz. A 2.727 and Toulouse 252.
Guilelmus Petrus de Falgar, *Quodlibeta*, MSS Brugges, Bibl. Comm. 185 and Paris, Bibl. Nat. lat. 14305.
Guilelmus Varronis, *Super sententias*, MSS Rome, Vat. lat. 4300; Padova, Antoniana 115 and 116; Oxford, Merton 103.
Humbertus de Prulliaco, *Super sententias*, MS Oxford, Bodl. Hatton 94.
Iohannes de Erfordia, *Super sententias*, MS Lüneburg Cod. theol. 2° 19.
Iohannes de Pecham, *Quaestiones de eucharistia*, MS Florence, Bibl. Naz. J 1.3.
Matthaeus de Aquasparta, *Quodlibeta*, MSS Assisi, Bibl. Comm. 134 and Todi, Bibl. Comm. 44.
——, *Super sententias*, MS Assisi, Bibl. Comm. 132.
Nicholas Ockham, *In sententiarum libros quattuor commentarius*, MS Oxford, Merton 134.
Petrus Iohannis Olivi, *Lectura super apocalypsim*, MS Rome, Bibl. Ang. 382.
——, *Quaestiones de perfectione evangelica*, q. 8, MS Rome, Vat. lat. 4986.
——, *Tractatus de sacramentis*, MSS Rome, Vat. lat. 4986 and Rome, Vat. Borgh. 13.
——, *Tractatus de usu paupere*, MS Rome, Vat. lat. 4986.
Petrus de Trabibus, *Super sententias*, MS Florence, Bibl. Naz. Conv. sopp. A 5.1071.
Raymundus Rigaldi, *Quodlibeta*, MS Todi, Bibl. Comm. 98.
Richardus Fishacre, *Super sententias*, MS Oxford, Oriel 43.

PUBLISHED PRIMARY SOURCES

Abbaudus, *Tractatus de fractione corporis Christi*, in *PL* 166, 1341–48.
Aegidius Romanus, *Errores philosophorum*, Milwaukee, Marquette University Press, 1944.
——, *In libros de physico auditu . . . eiusdem quaestio de gradibus formarum*, Venice, 1502.
——, *Theoremata de corpore Christi*, Bologna, 1481.
Albertus Magnus, *Commentarii in quartum librum sententiarum*, in *Opera*, Paris, Vivès, 1894, vol. 29.
——, *De sacramentis*, in *Opera*, Münster i. Westf., Aschendorff, 1958, vol. 26.
——, *Liber de sacramento eucharistiae*, in *Opera*, Paris, Vivès, 1899, vol. 38.
Augustinus, *De diversis quaestionibus*, in *PL* 40.
Bonaventura, *Breviloquium*, in *Opera*, Quaracchi, College of Saint Bonaventure, 1891, vol. 5.
——, *Commentarius in I, II, III, IV librum sententiarum*, in *Opera*, vol. 4.
Chartularium universitatis parisiensis, Bruxelles, Culture et Civilization, 1964.
Conciliorum oecumenicorum decreta, Bologna, Herder, 1962.
Gaufredus de Fontibus, *Quodlibeta*, in *Les Philosophes du Moyen Age*, vols. 2 and 3, Louvain and Paris, Institut Superieur de Philosophie de l'Université, 1904 and 1914.
——, *Les Quodlibets onze-quatorze de Godefroid de Fontaines*, in *Les Philosophes Belges*, vol. 5, fasc. 1–2, Louvain, Editions de l'Institut Superieur de Philosophie, 1932.
Gualterus de Bruges, *Le Questioni sull'eucaristia di Gualtiero di Bruges, O.F.M., 1225–1307*, Rome, Edizioni Francescane, 1962.

Guillelmus de Alvernia, *De sacramentis*, in *Opera*, Paris, Pralard, 1674, vol. 1.
Guilelmus de la Mare, *Correctorium fratris Thomae*, in *Correctorium corruptorii "quare"*, Kain, Le Saulchoir, 1927.
——, *Declarationes*, Münster i. W., Aschendorff, 1956.
Guilelmus de Militona, *Quaestiones de sacramentis*, Quaracchi, College of St. Bonaventure, 1961.
Guitmundus Aversanus, *De corporis et sanguinis Christi veritate*, in *PL* 149.
Henricus de Gandavo, *Quodlibeta*, Venice, Iacobus de Franciscis, 1613.
Hugo de Argentina, *Compendium theologiae veritatis*, in Albertus Magnus, *Opera*, Paris, Vivès, 1895, vol. 34.
Hugo de Sancto Victore, *De sacramentis*, in *PL* 176.
Innocentius III, *De sacro altaris mysterio libri sex*, in *PL* 217.
Iohannes de Bassolis, *In librum sententiarum opus*, Paris, 1517.
Iohannes Duns Scotus, *God and Creatures*, Princeton, University Press, 1975.
——, *Opus Oxoniense*, in *Opera*, Lyons, Laurentius Durand, 1639, vol. 8.
——, *Quaestiones quodlibetales*, St. Bonaventure, Franciscan Institute, 1950.
——, *Reportata Parisiensia*, in *Opera*, Lyons, Laurentius Durand, 1639, vol. 11.
——, *Reportata super primum . . . (quartum) sententiarum*, Paris, J. Granion, 1517–18.
Iohannes de Pecham, *Fratris Johannis Pecham . . . tractatus tres de paupertate*, Aberdeen, Typis Academicis, 1910.
——, *Johannis Pechami Quaestiones tractantes de anima*, Münster i. W., Aschendorff, 1918.
——, *Quodlibet Romanum*, Rome, Spicelegium Pontificii Athenaei Antoniani, 1938.
——, *Registrum epistolarum*, London, Longman, 1882–1885.
Littera septem sigillarum, in *AFH*, 47 (1954), 45–53.
Matthaeus de Aquasparta, *Quaestiones disputatae de incarnatione et de lapsu aliaeque selectae de Christo et de eucharistia*, Quaracchi, College of St. Bonaventure, 1957.
——, *Quaestiones disputatae de gratia*, Quaracchi, College of St. Bonaventure, 1935.
Petrus Iohannis Olivi, *Quodlibeta*, Venice, 1509.
——, *Tria scripta apologetica*, in *AFH*, 28 (1935), 115–55, 374–407; 29 (1936), 98–141, 365–95.
Petrus de Tarantasia, *In IV libris sententiarum commentaria*, Toulouse, Arnoldus Colomerius, 1652.
Richardus de Mediavilla, *Commentum super quarto sententiarum*, Venice, Dionysius Bertochus, 1489.
——, *Quaestio fratris Richardi de gradu formarum*, in Roberto Zavalloni, *Richard de Mediavilla et la controverse sur la pluralité des formes*, Louvain, Institut Superieur de Philosophie, 1951, 62–167.
——, *Quodlibeta*, Brescia, 1591.
Roger Marston, *Fr. Rogeri Marston O.F.M. Quodlibeta quatuor*, Quaracchi, College of St. Bonaventure, 1968.
Thomas Aquinas, *Commentaria in octo libros physicorum Aristotelis*, in *Opera*, Rome, Typographia Polyglotta, 1884, vol. 2.
——, *Quaestiones quodlibetales*, Taurini-Rome, Marietti, 1949.
——, *Summa contra gentiles*, in *Opera*, Rome, Typographia Polyglotta, 1918, vol. 12.
——, *Summa theologiae*, London, Eyre and Spottiswoode, 1964.
——, *Scriptum super sententias*, Paris, Lethielleux, 1947.
——, *Super epistolas S. Pauli lectura*, Taurini-Rome, Marietti, 1953.
——, *Super evangelium Matthaei lectura*, Taurini-Rome, Marietti, 1951.
——, *Super evangelium S. Ioannis lectura*, Taurini-Rome, Marietti, 1952.
Vitalis de Furno, *Quodlibeta tria*, Rome, Spicelegium Pontificii Athenaei Antoniani, 1947.

SECONDARY SOURCES

Balić, Charles, *Les Commentaires de Jean Duns Scot sur les quatre libres des Sentences*, Louvain, Bureaux de la Revue, 1927.
——, "The Life and Works of John Duns Scotus," *John Duns Scotus, 1265–1965*, Washington, D.C., Catholic University of America Press, 1965, 1–27.
Bettini, Orazio, "Olivi di fronte ad Aristotle," *Studi Francescani*, 55 (1958), 176–97.
Bettoni, Efrem, "Matteo d'Aquasparta e il suo posto nella scolastica post-tomistica," *Filosofia e cultura in Umbria tra Medioevo e Rinascimento*, Perugia, Centro di Studi Umbri, 1967, 231–48.

Bittremieux, J., "De transsubstantiatione quid sentierit S. Bonaventura," *Collectanea Franciscana,* 3 (1933), 26–39.

Bonner, Georg, "Über den dominikaner theologen Hugo von Strassburg," *Archivum fratrum praedicatorum,* 24 (1954), 269–86.

Brady, Ignatius, "John Pecham and the Background of Aquinas' De aeternitate mundi," *St. Thomas Aquinas, 1274–1974,* Toronto, Pontifical Institute of Mediaeval Studies, 1974, vol. 2, 141–78.

Brady, Ignatius, "Questions at Paris, c. 1260–1270," *Archivum Franciscanum Historicum,* 61 (1968), 434–61; 62 (1969), 357–76, 678–92.

Brampton, C. K., "Duns Scotus at Oxford, 1288–1301," *Franciscan Studies,* 24 (1964), 5–20.

Burr, David, "The Apocalyptic Element in Olivi's Critique of Aristotle," *Church History,* 40 (1979), 15–29.

——, "Ockham, Scotus, and the Censure at Avignon," *Church History,* 37 (1968), 144–59.

——, "Olivi and Baptismal Grace," *FS,* 57 (1975), 1–24.

——, *The Persecution of Peter Olivi,* in *American Philosophical Society Transactions,* vol. 66, part 5, Philadelphia, American Philosophical Society, 1976.

——, "Quantity and Eucharistic Presence: The Debate from Olivi through Ockham," *Collectanea Franciscana,* 44 (1974), 5–44.

——, "Scotus and Transubstantiation," *Mediaeval Studies,* 34 (1972), 336–50.

Buytaert, Eligius, "Circa doctrinam Duns Scoti de traditione et de Scripturae sufficientia adnotationes," *Antonianum,* 40 (1965), 346–62.

Callus, D. A., *The Condemnation of St. Thomas at Oxford,* London, Blackfriars, 1955.

——, "Introduction of Aristotelian Learning at Oxford," *Proceedings of the British Academy,* 29 (1943), 229–81.

Callebaut, A., "Le bx. Jean Duns Scot étudiant à Paris," *AFH,* 17 (1924), 3–12.

——, "Le maîtrise du Bx. Jean Duns Scot en 1305," *AFH,* 21 (1928), 206–39.

Creytins, R., "Pierre de Tarentaise, Professeur à Paris et Prieur Provincial de France," *Beatus Innocentius PP. V,* Rome, Vatican, 1943, 73–100.

Crowley, Theodore, "St. Bonaventure's Chronology Reappraisal," *FS,* 16 (1974), 310–22.

Daniels, Augustinus, "Zu den Beziehungen zwischen Wilhelm von Ware und Johannes Duns Scotus," *FS,* 4 (1917), 221–38.

Dossat, Yves, "Les cathares dans les documents de l'inquisition," *Cathares en Languedoc,* Toulouse, Privat, 1968, 71–104.

Doucet, Victorinus, "Quaestiones centum ad scholam franciscanam," *AFH,* 26 (1933), 183–202, 474–96.

Douie, Decima, *Archbishop Pecham,* Oxford, Clarendon Press, 1952.

Emden, Alfred B., *Biographical Register of the University of Oxford to 1500,* Oxford, Clarendon Press, 1957.

Emmen, Aquilinus, "Nicolas von Ockham," *LTK* 7.

——, "Wilhelm von Ware," *LTK* 10.

Fontaine, Raymond G., *Subsistent Accident in the Philosophy of Saint Thomas Aquinas and his Predecessors,* Washington, D.C., Catholic University of America Press, 1950.

Gál, Gedeon, "Gulielmi de Ware, O.F.M., doctrina philosophica per summa capita proposita," *Franciscan Studies,* 14 (1954), 155–80, 265–92.

Gandillac, M. de, *Histoire de l'Église,* vol. 13: *Le Mouvement doctrinal de XI au XIV siècle,* Paris, Bloud and Gay, 1951.

Gibson, Margaret, *Lanfranc of Bec,* Oxford, Clarendon Press, 1978.

Glorieux, Palemon, "D'Alexandre de Hales à Pierre Auriol," *AFH,* 26 (1933), 257–81.

——, *La literature quodlibetique,* Kain, Le Saulchoir, 1925 (vol. 1) and Paris, J. Vrin, 1935 (vol. 2).

——, "Maîtres franciscains régents à Paris," *Recherches de théologie ancienne et médiévale,* 18 (1951), 324–32.

——, "Sermons universitaires parisiens de 1267–68," *Recherches de théologie ancienne et médiévale,* 16 (1949), 51–58.

Grabmann, "Humbertus de Prulliaco (d. 1298), O. Cist. abbatis de Prulliaco quaestio de esse et essentia," *Angelicum,* 17 (1940), 352–69.

Harkins, Conrad, "The Authorship of a Commentary on the Franciscan Rule published among the Works of St. Bonaventure," *Franciscan Studies,* 29 (1969), 157–248.

Heynck, Valens, "Studien zu Johannes von Erfurt," *FS,* 40 (1958), 329–60; 42 (1960), 163–96.

——, "Vitalis de Furno," *LTK* 10.

——, "Zur Busslehre des Vitalis de Furno," *FS,* 41 (1959), 163–213.

——, "Zur Datierung der Sentenzenkommentare des Petrus Johannis Olivi und Petrus de Trabibus," *FS*, 38 (1956), 371–98.

——, "Zur Datierung einiger Schriften des Petrus Johannis Olivi," *FS*, 46 (1964), 335–64.

Hissette, Roland, *Enquête sur les 291 articles condamnées à Paris le 7 Mars 1277*, Louvain, Publications Universitaires and Paris, Vander-Oyez, 1977.

Hocedez, Edgar, *Richard de Middleton*, Louvain, Spicelegium Sacrum Louvaniense, and Paris, Édouard Champion, 1925.

Hödl, Ludwig, "Die confessio Berengarii von 1059," *Scholastik*, 37 (1962), 370–94.

——, "Der Transsubstantiationsbegriff in der scholastischen Theologie des 12. Jahrhunderts," *Recherches de théologie ancienne et médiévale*, 31 (1964), 230–59.

Iserloh, Erwin, "Abendmahl und Opfer in katholischer Sicht," *Abendmahl und Opfer*, Stuttgart, Schwabenverlag, 1960, 75–109.

Jorissen, H., *Die Entfaltung der Transsubstantiationslehre bis zum Beginn der Hochscholastik*, Münster, Aschendorff, 1965.

Kattum, Fr., *Die Eucharistielehre des heiligen Bonaventura*, Munich, 1920.

Koch, Joseph, "Die Verurteilung Olivis auf dem Konzil von Vienne und ihre Vorgeschichte," *Scholastik*, V (1930), 489–522.

Lampen, W., "B. Ioannes Duns Scotus, lector coloniensis," *Collectanea Franciscana Neerlandica*, 2 (1931), 297–300.

Lang, Albert, "Zur Eucharistielehre des hl. Albertus Magnus," *Divus Thomas* (Fr.), 19 (1932), 124–32.

Laurent, M.-H., *Le bienheureux Innocent V (Pierre de Tarentaise) et son temps*, Rome, Biblioteca Apostolica Vaticana, 1947.

Lechner, Joseph, "Die mehrfachen Fassungen des Sentenzenkommentars des Wilhelm von Ware, O.F.M." *FS*, 3 (1949), 14–31.

Little, A. G., "Chronological Notes on the Life of Duns Scotus," *English Historical Review*, 47 (1932), 368–82.

——, "The Franciscan School at Oxford," *AFH*, 19 (1926), 803–74.

Longpré, Ephrem, "Maîtres Franciscaines de Paris, Guillaume de Ware," *La France Franciscaine*, 15 (1922), 71–82.

Lottin, Odon, *Psychologie et morale aux XIIe et XIIIe siècles*, Gembloux, Duculot, 1960.

MacDonald, A. J., *Berengar and the Reform of Sacramental Doctrine*, London, New York and Toronto, Longmans, Green and Company, 1930.

Merlo, Grado G., *Eretici e inquisitori nella societa piemontese del trecento*, Torino, Claudiana, 1977.

Montclos, Jean de, *Lanfranc et Berenger*, Leuven, Spicelegium Sacrum Lovaniense, 1971.

Muller, J. P., "Wilhelm de la Mare," *LTK* 10.

Neunheuser, Burkhard, *Eucharistie in Mittelalter und Neuzeit*, Freiburg, Herder, 1963.

Nocke, Franz-Josef, *Sakrament und personaler Vollzug bei Albertus Magnus*, Münster, Aschendorff, 1967.

Paulus, J., *Henri de Gand*, Paris, J. Vrin, 1938.

Pelster, Franz, "Einige erganzende Angaben zum Leben und zu den Schriften des Wilhelm de la Mare OFM," *FS*, 37 (1955), 75–80.

——, "Les 'Declarations' et les questions de Guillaume de la Mare," *Recherches de théologie ancienne et médiévale*, 3 (1931), 397–411.

——, "Das Leben und die Schriften des Oxforder Dominikanerlehrers Richard Fishacre," *Zeitschrift für katholische Theologie*, 54 (1930), 518–53.

——, "Die Quaestionen des Alexander von Hales," *Gregorianum*, 14 (1933), 401–22, 501–20.

——, Review of H. Spettmann, "Pechams Kommentar" (see below), *Scholastik*, 3 (1928), 447.

Pfleger, Luzian, "Der dominikaner Hugo von Strassburg und das Compendium theologicae veritatis," *Zeitschrift für katholische Theologie*, 28 (1904), 429–40.

Plotnik, Kenneth, *Hervaeus Natalis OP and the Controversies over the Real Presence and Transubstantiation*, Munich, Paderborn and Vienna, Ferdinand Schöningh, 1970.

Quinn, John, "Chronology of St. Bonaventure (1217–1257)," *Franciscan Studies*, 10 (1972), 168–86.

Roensch, Frederick J., *The Early Thomistic School*, Dubuque, Priory Press, 1964.

Seeberg, Reinhold, *Lehrbuch der Dogmengeschichte*, Graz, Akademische Druk-u. Verlagsanstalt, 1953–54.

——, *Die Theologie des Johannes Duns Scotus*, Leipzig, Dietrich'sche Verlags-Buchhandlung, T. Weicher, 1900.

Sheedy, Charles E., *The Eucharistic Controversy of the Eleventh Century*, Washington, D.C., Catholic University of America Press, 1947.

Simonin, M.-D., "Les écrits de Pierre de Tarentaise," *Beatus Innocentius PP. V.*, Rome, Vatican, 1943, 163–335.

Spettmann, H., "Pechams Kommentar zum vierten Buch der Sentenzen," *Zeitschrift für katholische Theologie*, 52 (1928), 64–74.

Storff, Hugolinus, *De natura transubstantiationis iuxta I. Duns Scotum*, Quaracchi, College of St. Bonaventure, 1936.

Sylla, Edith, "Autonomous and Handmaiden Science," *The Cultural Context of Medieval Learning*, Dordrecht and Boston, D. Reidel, 1975, 349–96.

Vellico, Antonius, "De transsubstantiatione iuxta Ioannem Duns Scotum," *Antonianum*, 5 (1930), 301–32.

Weisheipl, James, *Friar Thomas d'Aquino*, Garden City, Doubleday, 1974.

Williams, Germain C., *The Nature of the Eucharistic Accidents*, Washington, D.C., Catholic University of America Press, 1951.

Wippel, John F., "The Condemnations of 1270 and 1277 at Paris," *Journal of Medieval and Renaissance Studies*, 7 (1977), 169–201.

Zavalloni, Roberto, *Richard de Mediavilla et la controverse sur la pluralité des formes*, Louvain, Institut Superieur de Philosophie, 1951.

INDEX OF PROPER NAMES